CELEBRATING HOLIDAYS AND HOLY DAYS

IN CHURCH AND FAMILY SETTINGS

Judy Weaver

DISCIPLESHIP RESOURCES

MATERIALS FOR GROWTH IN CHRISTIAN FAITH AND LIFE

P.O. Box 189 • Nashville, TN 37202 • Phone (615) 340-7285

*To Wendy, my granddaughter who lives far away,
I offer these celebrations for her family.*

Cover design by Ann L. Cummings.

Text illustrations by Alan Beam.

Library of Congress Catalog Card No. 88-51767

ISBN 0-88177-070-1

DR070B

CONTENTS

INTRODUCTION

Children live in a far different world than a generation ago. They are surrounded by conflicting value systems and bombarded by the images and violence which television teaches. Each day, commercials tell them what they should do, own, and be. Family communication most often consists of TV viewing with conversation limited to station breaks and commercial times. Often both parents are employed, and children are at home alone afternoons, sometimes frightened behind locked doors; or their free time is so programmed into competitive sports, music, and dance lessons that there is little or no time left for creative play or daydreaming, so essential to a child's growth.

In addition, many families are split and children have, instead of two parents, four or one. Extended family members, grandparents, cousins, aunts, and uncles live far away from each other and indeed aren't even known. A sense of family history and vital tradition is lost. Role models and value systems were previously developed within these settings from lengthy conversations and experiences together. The establishment of rituals and traditions around holidays and special days was a vital part of knowing one another and living in the same community. Today these traditions have been abandoned.

Contrast today's world with the setting in which I was raised in a mid-sized city in Massachusetts. Relatives lived nearby, and we met together for all major holidays and many times in-between for spontaneous cookouts and parties. Cousins became best friends; aunts and uncles were special confidants. As we gathered, we knew which traditional foods would be served and what rituals observed, but we also established ties with the past and a confidence for the future.

When we are in danger of losing our rituals and traditions, we must write them down. This book is needed because church participation is no longer an every week event. Many other activities take prime time, leaving church to left-over times when there is nothing else to do. Here, too, traditions and rituals are transient, often changing with each turnover of pastor or other staff. Children are often no longer participants in total church events. Activities such as whole families assisting in clean-up days or working together to package food for mission projects are now taken on by select groups, often leaving children uninvolved. In Sunday school, teachers teach every other week or are rotated frequently. Children don't get to know a teacher as role model and, indeed, the attendance is often as erratic as their leaders'. Long-term projects and activities have become a thing of the past.

In writing about holidays, I intend to assist churches, classroom teachers, and parents in reestablishing sacred traditioning as part of being together and celebrating holy days and special days. Background information is given for each day, followed by a section for Sunday school, worship, or other church settings. Some of these activities involve whole congregations together, others are for individuals or groups of classes. At times I have listed activities appropriate during worship and Sunday school hours; but at other times activities are given for evenings, weekends, or overnight experiences in the expectation that teachers will commit to greater involvement, so that children and adults will, over time, come to know and learn from each other.

A section on Jewish holidays has also been included because children and adults need to learn more about the roots from which Christianity comes and about the Jewish community which is such an influential part of American life.

The third section for each day is intended for families, because they, too, need to spend time with each other. Conversation starters, activities, worship settings, and recipes are included. Children should participate fully in all areas of family celebrations, so many recipes are deliberately simple to allow them involvement in food preparation. The word *family* as used in this book is intended to include single-parent families as well as extended family settings. In some cases I have suggested inviting other relatives, neighbors, or friends to participate in order to enlarge a small family setting as well as to broaden the sphere of influential persons in the child's life.

Masculine terminology has been used in the Declaration of Independence because it is the historically correct term there, and sometimes activities are suggested as possibly different for boys and girls. This is not intended to be sexist, but it is to recognize differences. However, boys and girls should always feel free to do what activities they choose.

The term *Indians* is used in the historical sense because that is the name by which they were known by early settlers. I have changed it to Native Americans when speaking of them in the present, to recognize that this is the term usually used today.

In no area has the intent been to program families into these definite patterns of celebrations, but rather this book is written to stimulate you to establish or reestablish traditions which shall become sacred to you.

NEW YEAR'S DAY JANUARY 1

Celebrations of this holiday are very ancient and almost universal around the world. The Babylonians some 3,000 years before Christ held annual eleven-day celebrations, an *akitu*, with ceremonies of purification and rituals to ancient gods. Egyptians and Persians celebrated it in September at the autumnal equinox, while the Greeks preferred December 21 or the winter solstice. To the Jews the first month of Tishri (in September) was the New Year and known as Rosh Hashanah. In America, the Iroquois and Huron tribes celebrated the holiday each year some time between January and March, varying the date as it suited them.

Finally, Julius Caesar chose January for the beginning of the calendar year and named it in honor of the god Janus, who, because he had two faces, was able to look back and forward, presumably into two years.

Pope Gregory XIII revised the Julian calendar to the one we use today, now called the Gregorian calendar. Roman Catholic countries immediately adopted it. Among Protestants caught in the Reformation, however, it rang too much of papal influence. Therefore it wasn't until the 1700s that most European countries accepted this calendar and, presumably along with it, the celebration of the New Year.

Throughout history this holiday has included many strange and interesting rituals from rites of purification and confession of sins to extinguishing and rekindling fires, masked processions, carnivals, wild orgies, and gift giving. In many cultures it is linked with new fertility for the dormant land.

It has always been a time for noisemaking with horns, ringing the bells, shouting and firecrackers, dating way back into its history. For a period of time, sticks were used to beat out the old and beat in the new year. In England this graduated to a beating on apple trees accompanied by music in order to urge the trees to produce a large crop in the coming months.

New Year's gift giving, everything from exchanging eggs in ancient Persia, to giving pins, gloves, and extravagant gifts to royalty, have been a special part of the day. The custom was stopped in England by the Puritans and this has largely halted the custom to the present day, except in some Latin American countries where it continues.

The early Christian church, disturbed by the paganism of New

1

Year's Day, declared January first as the Feast of the Circumcision in
A.D. 487, to commemorate Jesus' circumcision. It is also called Jesus'
Name Day. Luke 2:21 tells about this circumcision, and verses 22-38
tell of his presentation at the temple and include the story of Simeon
and Anna.

The Wassail Carol is a part of this day, and the word comes from
two old Gaelic words *was hael,* meaning good health. Wassail cakes
and drinks in Great Britain are still a part of the celebrating, as is the
singing of the song.

In the United States it is hardly the New Year until the strains of
"Auld Lang Syne," a song of sadness and reflection, have been played
on radio and television. This day has been associated with new beginnings, resolutions, and good luck charms. A custom of "dipping"
in the Bible prevailed in some parts of Europe and early America
where the head of a household would open the Bible first thing New
Year's Day, run his finger down a page, and choose a verse which
would reflect his fortune in the coming year.

In Germany many people cut six onions in half, scooped out the
insides, filled them with salt, named them for each month and left
them in the attic. The ones in which the salt dissolved predicted
which months would be dry ones in the year ahead, as they antici-
pated new crops.

Early American presidents held open house on this day, inviting
friends and dignitaries to dine. Thomas Jefferson included chiefs of
the Cherokee nation in his New Year's celebration.

Today this day has become known for the Pasadena Rose Parade
and colorful football games throughout the land. In some churches it
is marked with watch night services and the serving of communion,
with its promise of new beginnings and new commitments to the
faith.

NEW YEAR'S CELEBRATION IN
SUNDAY SCHOOL SETTINGS

Begin class time with the stories of Jesus' presentation at the
temple, the sacrifice of two young pigeons, and his meeting of Simeon
and Anna. Often these stories are not a part of regular Sunday school
curriculum. Point out to the children that the gift of two pigeons

indicates the poverty of Mary and Joseph but also their faithfulness as Jews to follow the rituals designated for new babies. Share the meaning and importance of Jesus in all of our lives. As a class, write out ways to fulfill that importance with New Year's PROMISES. These may be slipped into toilet paper rolls, covered with tissue paper, tied with ribbons and stored by the teacher until some time later in the year when they will be returned for each child to read and evaluate.

This is a good time to make CALENDARS to take home. A painting done by each child with the monthly dates purchased at a stationery store and attached to the picture could hang on a wall at home. Small desk calendars can be also made with a Polaroid picture of each child attached to a folded piece of poster board and a small calendar attached.

Winter picture CARDS of snowmen made with cotton balls and construction paper delivered to nursing homes will be welcomed by the patients there.

New Year's party HATS for a class or home party can be made with a piece of construction paper 11″ long by 6″ wide. Attach the two long ends together, forming a peak or a lopsided cone. The outside may be decorated with paint, glitter, and confetti.

CASCARONES are a Mexican happy day symbol which are fun at this time of year. When preparing eggs at home, for several weeks before class time, break an egg carefully at the smaller end, removing the insides. Openings should be as small as possible—¾″ will be large enough to remove the egg easily and also to refill it. Wash the inside and allow it to dry, fill it with confetti, and tape it shut. Children may then paint the outside with pretty colors and designs. When dried, these are broken on the heads of friends as love gifts.

Noisemakers can be made of buttons or small pebbles in juice cans or other small containers, wrapped with the paper and decorated. Your party might be held on New Year's Eve (an overnighter is fun) or some other time during the Christmas school break.

NEW YEAR'S IN FAMILY SETTINGS

This is an excellent holiday to enjoy with children, to establish family traditions, and forego the traditional, meaningless holiday parties. Most people celebrate this holiday on New Year's Eve, reserving the following day for a quieter time. Enjoy the evening meal together—perhaps a fondue supper of beef chunks dipped in oil in the FONDUE pot—peanut oil is best for this. Have a variety of sauces for the meat: a barbecue sauce, teriyaki sauce, and whatever other sauce your family enjoys. Salad, baked potatoes, and a vegetable can complete the meal. A dessert of your choice—perhaps ice cream—can come next. However, include fortune cookies just for fun and because the quest for one's fortune fits with the season.

As part of the family time together, each family member should write down RESOLUTIONS for the coming year, four or more promises to try to keep. Each family member can put these in an envelope and seal it. Then seal all envelopes with a sealing wax kit which many children own. The person's name needs to be on the envelope. These should be packed away until next New Year's Eve when they are to be opened, read, and shared.

Since this is also the Name of Jesus or Circumcism Day, it might be a time to reflect on the NAMES of each member of the family. Children like to know how they came to receive the name they have, what the name means—and perhaps the history of the family name. An exchange of some inexpensive name gifts (pens, cups, pins, etc.) can be done.

Party hats and noisemakers would also be fun for children, and family members could play games together. For a midnight snack, if anyone remains up that late, sponge cake and wassail are traditional and delicious.

Wassail

6	c. apple juice or cider	3	tbl. lemon juice
1	cinnamon stick	1	tsp. lemon rind
¼	tsp. nutmeg	2½	c. unsweetened pineapple
¼	c. honey or 2 tbl. brown		juice
	sugar		

Heat apple juice and cinnamon stick. Bring to a boil and simmer for five minutes. Add the remaining ingredients and simmer uncovered five minutes longer. Keep warm over low heat. Serves twenty.

New Year's Day might be a good time to eat whatever leftover turkey there is. Here is a wonderful recipe for this.

Turkey Paprikish with Dumplings

¼ c. butter	1 tbl. Worcestershire sauce
3 lbs. turkey and dressing, chopped up	3 tbl. chopped parsley
	2 tsp. paprika
1 tsp. seasoned salt	¼ c. chopped onion
1 c. water	

Melt butter. Add remaining ingredients, cover and simmer for thirty minutes. Add more water if it is needed.

Dumplings

2 c. sifted flour	2 eggs
4 tsp. baking powder	½ c. milk
1 tsp. seasoned salt	1 tbl. chopped parsley

Combine all ingredients and stir until smooth and stiff. After turkey has simmered, drop large spoonsful of dumpling mixture on top of the meat mixture, cover and allow it to steam for ten minutes. Turn dumplings to one side and, if needed, cook an additional five minutes. Remove dumplings and add 1½ cups sour cream to the meat mixture. Warm slightly—and dish is ready to serve. Makes 4-6 servings.

EPIPHANY JANUARY 6

"In those days Jesus came from Nazareth of Galilee and was baptized by John in the Jordan" (Mark 1:9). This scripture marks the first of three traditions which are associated with Epiphany. As early as the second century, January 6 was believed to be the day of Jesus' baptism and was so stated in the writings of Clement of Alexandria. It is known that, by the fourth century in Palestine, both the birth and baptism of Jesus were celebrated on this day. The blessing of the Nile, an ancient heathen festival, was held in Egypt January 6; and it is believed the early church thus adopted it as the time of the Baptism. Indeed, separate traditions throughout history have held that waters drawn on Epiphany are sacred, possess special healing powers, and will remain pure longer than other waters. The Greek Orthodox Church continues to honor Jesus' baptism and in some parts of the world holds ceremonies where they bless the waters of oceans, rivers, and lakes and even release a dove to fly overhead. Matthew 3:3-17 gives a more complete account of Jesus' baptism.

A second ancient celebration connected to this day is of the wedding in Cana described in John 2:1-11 when Jesus is said to have turned water into wine. Probably again the Greek Orthodox Church is most noted for recognition of this event on this day.

However, the Western church celebrates it as the traditional time of the visit of the wise men to the infant Jesus. Since they were strangers from far-off lands, Epiphany symbolizes spreading of the light of Jesus to the whole world. Many fascinating and curious legends have surrounded the story of the wise men as found in Matthew 2. Although the Bible never says how many there were, tradition finally settled on three wise men as the proper number since there are three gifts mentioned. (As few as two and as many as twelve have been given as the correct number also.)

During the ninth century, names were given to these men; and they were promoted from wise men (thought to be astrologers) to kings, which is not mentioned in the Bible story: Caspar, King of Tarsus, the land of myrrh; Melchior, King of Arabia, place of gold; and Balthasar, King of Sheba, known for having frankincense. A further symbolism in the gifts developed, with gold representing the child as king, frankincense (an incense) standing for worship, and myrrh symbolizing Jesus' death because it is used in embalming.

6

It is not known how they traveled or came to be together, however both Spain and Italy developed legends of three kings journeying through their lands. In Italy they are believed to have passed the woman Befana (a shortened form of Epiphania), who was too busy sweeping to take notice of the magi, although she did hear them. Later she regretted missing an opportunity to visit the Christ child, and as punishment she was ordered by an angel to fill children's stockings each Epiphany eve. It seems she was resentful and on the first year filled them with ashes from her hearth. Later she repented and filled them correctly with gifts and food treats, giving ashes only to naughty children. This story symbolizes how gift giving came to be a part of Epiphany instead of Christmas in both Spain and Italy.

January 6 marked the end of the Advent season and the beginning of a carnival time which the early church celebrated through Shrove Tuesday or the beginning of Lent.

Medieval France celebrated this day with cakes in which a special bean was placed; the lucky person who found it would become king of the feast or party which followed, and everyone had to do his bidding. This tradition continues to this day in France.

England had a curious custom of lighting twelve fires, one for each disciple, all of which blazed high except Judas' which was stomped upon and extinguished. People then danced around the others in a large circle. They often served a twelfth day cake, drank cider, and ate a meal of beef, potatoes, and onions fried together.

In Norway it was the day to sweep the house clean of all Christmas items and to burn the greens used during the Christmas holiday. Star boys carrying stars on poles went through towns singing and acting out biblical stories.

Today "Amahl and the Night Visitors," another story of the wise men, is often acted out (however, usually before Christmas) and presented in churches. Songs such as "We Three Kings," "As with Gladness Men of Old," and "The Twelve Days of Christmas" are still traditional and are sung in churches or schools.

EPIPHANY IN SUNDAY SCHOOL SETTINGS

During class time, share the three different stories of Jesus related to this holiday: the visit of the wise men, his baptism, and the wedding at Cana. Children might make mobiles of SYMBOLS related to these

traditions: doves cut from styrofoam meat trays, rings or water jugs to symbolize the wedding at Cana, and crowns and a star for the story of the wise men. Symbols can then be attached to dowels with ribbon. Children could make one large mobile for the room or individual ones to take home. Children might also make banners of the wise men. A pattern is included.

Announce an Epiphany CLEANING PARTY for the next Saturday or Sunday morning. Invite children to come prepared to clean the classroom of all items related to Christmas—the tree, decorations, pictures, etc. Work on this should begin as soon as the first child arrives. The room might then be redecorated for the next unit of Sunday school curriculum. When you are satisfied the room is ready, begin the Epiphany party by retelling the story of the wise men and the legend of Befana of Italy.

Together make tagboard CROWNS and star poles. A cardboard star painted yellow with gold glitter added may be attached with a thumb-tack to a painted dowel. Epiphany LANTERNS may also be made by

folding an 8″ x 11″ piece of construction paper in half and making cuts along the fold approximately ½″ apart and 1½″ from the edges of the paper. Next open the paper and attach the two short sides of the paper together with glue or scotch tape. Make a handle ¾″ wide and approximately 6″ long. Attach the handle to the lantern.

Children can then dress in long robes, put on their crowns, and have a PARADE, carrying lanterns and star poles. If this party is held on a day when other classes are meeting, they might deliver wrapped candy treats to them or stop and tell Bible stories as children in Norway do at this time of year.

For refreshments, share frosted cupcakes and cider. Conclude the party by singing songs of the season.

EPIPHANY WORSHIP FOR HOME OR SUNDAY SCHOOL CLASS

Reader #1: Today is Epiphany, the day we remember the wise men who visited Jesus.

(Child unwraps the wise men and places them at the manger.)

Reader #2: Matthew 2:1-12.

Reader #1: This story tells us about men who traveled from far-off places, guided by a star, in search of the Messiah. Since they were foreigners, this story tells us that Jesus came to lead people all over the world to God: Jews, Gentiles, rich and poor alike.

Reader #3: *(Lights 3 candles)* We don't really know how many wise men visited Jesus. Three have been chosen because of the gifts which they brought. Gold represents to us that Jesus is King; frankincense was used in worship and symbolizes that we are to worship Jesus; myrrh, an ingredient used in embalming, reminds us that Jesus died for us.

Reader #2: Jesus came to show the world and each of us how to love others and follow God. It is important for each of us to try to do that every day.

Sing or say all together words of "We Three Kings of Orient Are."

Closing prayer: Cleanse our hearts, O Lord, that we might be worthy of your love. Forgive us when we are not kind to one another and lead us in new directions so that we might be filled with joy and love. In Jesus' name we pray. Amen.

EPIPHANY IN FAMILY SETTINGS

Since this day celebrates three distinctly different experiences in Jesus' life, here is an opportunity for your family to explore each one. Reading about events from the Bible followed by conversation is a good way to do this.

The story of Jesus' baptism is told in Matthew 3:1-17. After reading, children might like to hear again about their own baptism and see photos and other memorabilia. If they have godparents, a phone call or letter and an invitation to dinner (if they are nearby) might be appropriate. Share also the different ways in which people can be baptized—by sprinkling, pouring, or immersion. Perhaps you have not had your children baptized and are waiting until they are old enough to make this decision for themselves. If this is true, telling about your own baptism and the meaning of this experience can be shared instead. Talk with the pastor to learn when there will be a baptism as a part of worship, and plan to attend with the children so they can observe and learn.

In talking about the Wedding of Cana (found in John 2:1-11) parents might share the excitement of their wedding day and what being married means to them. If this is not possible, then a sharing of the value of what the present family means might be more appropriate.

The story of the wise men's visit to the infant Jesus (Matthew 2) tells the final story generally associated with the Christmas season. Share this together, plan a time for worship, light three candles to remember the wise men who traveled from far off to see the Christ child, and add the wise men to the crèche scene. The legend of Befana is interesting to tell; and leaving stockings for her to fill, as children in Spain and Italy do, might be an enjoyable new tradition for the family.

Last, prepare an Epiphany cake, dropping a coin or a bean inside before baking. The family member who discovers it may choose a one-day outing or trip for all the family to enjoy together.

Three Kings Bread

1 (16 oz.) package hot roll mix	1 egg
that contains yeast	½ tsp. allspice and cinnamon
1 c. hot tap water	

Prepare this part using the instructions on the package mix as a guide in mixing and kneading the bread. Cover the bowl, place in a warm place, and allow dough to rise for 30 minutes.

Filling:
  Cream together:

¼ c. margarine	1 c. chopped nuts
4 tbl. brown sugar	½ tsp. vanilla or almond extract
2 c. toasted coconut	

When dough has risen, roll it out on a floured board until about ½" to ¾" thick, spread filling all over the top, add the coin, and roll the bread together like a jelly roll. Place on a greased cookie sheet and let it rise an additional 30 minutes. Brush it with the white from one egg and bake 40 minutes at 375°. Place it on a rack to cool and serve.

MARTIN LUTHER KING DAY JANUARY

M. L., as he was known by his family, was born on January 15, 1929, in Atlanta, Georgia, where a couple of years later his father became the pastor of Ebenezer Baptist Church. M. L. was certainly an intelligent child. By the age of five he could recite whole Bible passages and sing entire songs from memory. As a preschooler, his closest playmate was a white boy; but by the time the two children entered separate schools, he was no longer allowed to be seen with him. Thus, he learned about discrimination at an early age. He was intuitively sensitive to his surroundings; people in bread lines or discriminated against in any way greatly disturbed him, and he declared that he would do something to correct it one day.

School was easy. M. L. started a year early, skipped some grades, and went on to Morehouse College. At this time he secured a summer job working on a Connecticut farm where he discovered blacks and whites could eat in the same restaurants and attend the same theaters. Segregation became more difficult for him when he returned home, and he determined to help change that. At first sociology was his major subject, but a kind teacher directed him toward religion, which had been the family's choice all along. He attended Crozer Seminary in Chester, Pennsylvania, again earning straight As. Here he learned of Gandhi's work in India, and Martin began to fashion his ideas from this great leader.

A Ph.D. was earned from Boston University, and M. L. returned with Coretta, his wife, to pastor Dexter Avenue Baptist Church in Montgomery. His congregation adored him. Under his direction, committees and political groups were formed to assist the needy. Soon he became known as a political activist.

When Mrs. Rosa Parks refused to move to the back of the bus as stated by law, Martin's leadership found its direction. An organized plan to boycott buses was the beginning of his true ministry. In all he did, nonviolence and peaceful demonstrations became his motto. A Supreme Court ruling finally led to open buses. By then he was nationally known.

As a speaker, he could captivate audiences. He was articulate, emotional, and always concerned for others. At one point in his ministry, he prayed that no one would have to die as a result of his struggle for civil rights and ended by adding that, if anyone should suffer, let it be himself. He couldn't continue the prayer and had to be led from the pulpit. Unfortunately violence did erupt at times: bombings occurred; crosses were burned; and people, including King, were jailed for their struggle.

Martin was able to secure better voting rights for blacks; to integrate schools, lunch counters, and buses; and to urge for better housing and jobs for all the poor. He worked through several Presidents but never felt that they moved fast enough to insure equal rights for all.

Though he kept an exhausting schedule for many years, he was able to write books, preach almost every other Sunday in his church, and accept numerous awards and prizes, including an honorary degree from Yale and the Nobel Peace prize. Martin sometimes complained that there was no time to write new speeches because he was speaking so often.

On April 3, 1968, he addressed a huge audience of followers in Memphis. There he spoke of having reached the mountaintop and he related death threats. Both incidents led people to speculate that he had a premonition. It was a fateful next evening when King was gunned down by James Earl Ray on a hotel balcony. It wasn't the first attempt on his life. His career almost ended years before in New York City when he was stabbed by an insane woman.

All over the world people responded to this tragedy. President Johnson declared Sunday, April 7, as a day of national mourning; flags flew at half mast, and Coretta and the children joined with 19,000 people in a silent march. Martin was buried in South View Cemetery near his beloved grandmother. On his crypt are printed these words, "Free at last, free at last; thank God almighty, I'm free at last."

A date in January close to his birthday (January 15) is chosen each year to celebrate his life. The holiday became nationally recognized in 1986, although not all states have honored it. In the spirit of M. L. King, there is still much to do on behalf of the poor and the oppressed.

MARTIN LUTHER KING DAY
IN SUNDAY SCHOOL

Children do learn about this holiday in school but may not receive much information about the religious purpose behind his life. Since he was named after another great reformer, Martin Luther, tell the class about his namesake. Discuss ways in which they were alike and ways in which they were different. Ask them if they think being named after someone important might lead a person to seek greatness. Invite each child to share something he/she already knows about Martin Luther King, Jr. Ask the children to name others who have died for a belief. Talk about Jesus, Gandhi, and King together and about the kind of faith and commitment one needs in order to be willing to die for a cause.

Another great religious leader was Moses, who led his people out of slavery in Egypt, through the wilderness to freedom in a new land. Make FRIEZE pictures of both leaders, comparing what each did.

Talk about problems in our country and in the world today which need correcting. List some of them. Cut out magazine pictures and newspaper headlines; glue some of them on a long sheet of butcher paper and hang it on the wall. Ask the question, "What are Christians doing today to correct these problems, and what can each of us do?"

Play a GAME of Love versus Hate. Needed: One large die which can be made from a square of plastic foam, and covered with flannel. Dots can be made on each side with a marking pen. Also needed is one package of 11"x16" construction paper. A number of blank pieces of paper will be interspersed beside others which have writing. The teacher can make up the writings or use ones which are suggested below. Papers will be placed like a game board all along the floor, beginning with "start" and ending with "finish." Children play by throwing the die and moving the correct number of spaces and doing what is written on the space. The first one to reach the finish space wins.

Ideas for sayings:

1. Start. 2. Lose a turn for not feeding a hungry person. 3. Go ahead two spaces for being kind. 4. Your offering to the poor was received, take an extra turn. 5. Go to the thinking chair for selfishness, lose a turn. 6. You didn't learn about loving, lose a turn. 7. Contribute a blanket to a shelter, go ahead one space. 8. Lose a turn for spending all your allowance on yourself. 9. You helped a friend today, go ahead one space. 10. Stay here and lose a turn unless you can recite the Golden Rule. 11. You visited someone who was sick, go ahead two spaces. 12. Say a Bible verse about love and have a second

turn. 13. Say what you will do to help the poor and avoid going back
4 spaces. 14. You ignored the church's request for an offering for the
hungry, lose two turns. 15. Finish line, winner's space. In addition to
spaces with instructions, at least an equal number of blank spaces
needs to be part of the game board.

After playing the game, talk together again about the significance
of Martin Luther King, Jr.'s life. Ask each class member what wrong
he or she thinks this leader would be trying to correct if he were still
alive today. Children might like to write a letter to someone in their
city or town, expressing concern for some issue or problem which
exists close by.

Close by saying together the prayer of St. Francis of Assissi.

Prayer of St. Francis

Lord, make me an instrument of Your Peace.
Where there is hatred, let me sow love;
Where there is injury, pardon;
Where there is doubt, faith;
Where there is despair, hope;
Where there is darkness, light;
Where there is sadness, joy;
O Divine Master, grant that I may seek not so much to be consoled as to
console; to be understood as to understand; to be loved as to love; for it is
in giving that we receive; it is in pardoning that we are pardoned; and it
is in dying that we are born to Eternal Life. Amen.

MARTIN LUTHER KING DAY IN FAMILIES

Most young parents today were either babies or small children
themselves when this man was still alive. You may recall some memories of him from newspapers or television, or perhaps you even
knew someone who met or marched with him. During a person's
lifetime we often fail to recognize his or her greatness. It was this way
for Martin Luther King, Jr. He threatened powerful people and often
was considered a lawbreaker and a troublemaker. It is important to
help children understand that the achievements of a person are often
understood more fully as one looks back on that life. Rent a VIDEO
tape or watch a television program about Martin Luther King, Jr., as
there will certainly be tributes given during the week preceding his
birthday.

Children do need to know that even today all is not fair and just in the world, and it is our responsibility to correct injustice wherever we find it. It's appropriate, too, to celebrate the fact that we live in a country where people who protest wrongs are eventually heard and where it is possible to bring about changes for the better—when people care enough to work for the greater good.

Discuss the evils of prejudice and the self-worth of all persons. Rejoice together that God created people of different races, talents, and abilities, and that we were all intended to live together in harmony and appreciation of each other's uniqueness. Pray together that one day all prejudice will end and that people everywhere will be valued for who they are and not how they look.

Enjoy a DINNER of "soul" food—blackeyed peas, collard greens with hamhocks, cornbread, and yam pie.

Hamhocks and Collard Greens

4	or 5 smoked hamhocks or	6	lb. collard greens
	1 lb. bacon		salt and sugar to taste
2½	quarts water		
1	tsp. crushed red pepper		

Simmer hamhocks in water with red pepper until tender (at least 2 hours). Wash the greens thoroughly and sprinkle them with salt. When meat is done, remove from the pot and cook greens in the pan juice, stirring occasionally to mix the ingredients. Season with sugar and salt and serve with cornbread.

Yam or Sweet Potato Pie

Prepare an unbaked pastry shell and heat oven to 425°.

5	c. cooked mashed yams	¼	tsp. allspice
1	c. evaporated milk	¼	tsp. ginger
¾	c. margarine (melted)		sprinkle of cloves
¾	c. brown sugar	3	eggs (beaten slightly)
½	c. granulated sugar	1½	tsp. vanilla
1¼	tsp. cinnamon		

Add margarine and sugars to the mashed yams, followed by all other ingredients. Mix well, and bake at 425° for approximately one hour or until set. (Yams do better in the pie since sweet potatoes present a greenish cast.)

VALENTINE'S DAY FEBRUARY 14

The origin of Valentine's Day is something of a mystery and not without controversy. One story—that it was named for a monk of the Roman Catholic Church who sent love notes to people outside his monastery—is considered a legend. In fact, there are at least two saints who bore the name of Valentine—one a priest of Rome, the second a bishop of Interamna. Both of these men were martyred for their faith. Of a third St. Valentine, little is known, but none of these men can really be associated with the holiday.

There was, however, an ancient Roman holiday called Lupercalia, a feast day in honor of the Roman gods, Juno and Pan, that was celebrated in mid-February. As a part of this holiday young women put their names into a box and young men drew them out to see for whom they were to be *gallant* (meaning lover of women). Each man was to pursue the woman whose name he drew with gifts and attention for the next year.

The day came to be called Galantin Day. Since *g*'s and *v*'s were often interchanged in ancient writing, this is probably how Valentine's Day came to be named.

Ancient Christian clergy objected to this pagan holiday and set about Christianizing it (since it was too popular to be eliminated). One legend says that they substituted the names of saints for women's names in the boxes, and when the men drew these names instead of a fine maiden's, they were charged with responsibility to spend the next year trying to emulate the saint whose name they drew.

The choice of February 14 revolves around a belief that it is on this day that birds begin to mate, and thus it was an appropriate time to think about love.

Many young women came to believe that the first person of the opposite sex whom they saw on this day would become their one true love. This practice caused many a young woman to keep her eyes closed until a suitable choice could be located.

We know that the holiday was celebrated in the fifteenth century when costume balls and greeting cards became a common custom of the day.

By Civil War times (USA), Valentine's Day was widely celebrated. For a period of years, comic valentines (often containing crude messages) were commonly distributed. However, by the twentieth cen-

18

tury the holiday became more of a children's celebration with the making and distributing of greeting cards in school.

Today post offices in such towns as Darling, Pennsylvania; Love, Mississippi; and Kissimee, Florida, do a huge business as mail is forwarded by people wanting a special postmark on their loved one's card.

VALENTINE'S DAY IDEAS FOR CHURCH SETTINGS

Valentine's Day is a time to think about love. Since the central theme of Jesus' ministry is love, it is an appropriate time to combine Christian teachings with a secular holiday.

In the Classroom

There are many Bible stories of love that can be used in church classroom settings. A few suggestions are the stories of Ruth or David and Jonathan, or the parables of the good Samaritan and the prodigal son. Also, many stories about Paul carry the theme of love.

VALENTINES can be made in all Sunday school classes with Bible verses about love glued onto them. (Look these up in a commentary and type them up small so that they can be cut out and attached to cards.) They may then be given away to every member of the congregation as they leave the worship service on the Sunday closest to Valentine's Day.

If your children are in worship the same time as adults, arrange for them to leave before the sermon to prepare a surprise for the congregation. Or do as our children's classes do: begin to make valentines three to four weeks early to be certain there are enough for every person who attends worship.

Valentines are best made by offering various sizes of heart patterns; putting out lace paper doilies; white, pink, and red paper stickers; tissue paper; ribbon; Bible verses; scissors; and paste. Children will create their own designs, but it's important to have a Bible verse on each one. It's fun also to have scalloping or pinking shears to cut out the hearts and give them an interesting shape. Cards can be made three-dimensional with a small piece of sponge cut out and glued to the back of a heart or other design and attaching it to the background.

Children can make a special valentine for parents by cutting out heart shapes of various sizes and making valentine people. A polaroid photo of the child's face can be placed on the head, adding a personal touch to the card. See the illustration.

Valentine MOBILES are fun and may be made by hanging hearts of various sizes on a wire coat hanger.

As a class, write a valentine love message to children in a nearby Sunday school. Be certain that all the children sign the message.

Involve children in a "love project for my church." Gather together on a Saturday to CLEAN UP and fix up around the property as a gift to the congregation. Children can clean cupboards, wash nursery toys, sharpen pew pencils, scrub finger marks off walls, and perform a variety of other chores. Please be certain that other members of the congregation recognize and thank the children appropriately for what they have done.

Have a CLASS PARTY on a Saturday in February. Invite all the children to wear something red and to bring valentines to exchange with other class members.

As children arrive, the boys may make valentine bow ties (two hearts joined together at the points). These may be pinned onto their shirts. The girls can make valentine HATS using a large paper plate. Cut out the center and glue hearts around the outside. Ribbons can tie the hats under the chin. Sing songs that express love to all the children together. ("Magic Penny" is a good choice.)

Have Bible verses about love printed on hearts ahead of time. Cut in half and give each child half of a heart. They must go around and find the other half of their heart. This person now becomes their PART-NER. They must memorize the Bible verse together and shout out, "Valentine!" when they can both say it. Continue the game until all children have found their partner and recited their verse.

Another GAME idea is to write down on cards names of famous persons who have a known love partner. Children will pair with their partner and draw a card. They must be able to name the love partner of the person whose name they draw within ten seconds. If they do so, they may keep the card. The team with the most cards at the end of the game wins. The names on the cards may be chosen from well-known members of the congregation, TV shows, biblical or famous people, or even comic strips. Names chosen need to be appropriate to the age level of the children.

Valentine People   ## Valentine Bookmark

Fun activities may also be a part of the party. Children might make a valentine TREE for a worship table decoration for the next morning's class (a tree branch with hearts and love Bible verses attached with tape or glue). Valentine gifts can also be made to take home. A bookmark made with a ribbon and lined with hearts is easy and quick to make.

A more complicated GIFT can be made with half of an embroidery hoop. Heart shapes cut from cardboard and covered with pretty cloth can be glued around the circle. A ribbon streamer can be added, along with a strip of lace around the outside of the hoop.

Enjoy heart-shaped SANDWICHES made with peanut butter and red jelly. Cut the bread into shapes with a cookie cutter. Serve a red drink and red apple slices.

A valentine CAKE will make a good dessert and may be made by putting red food coloring and maraschino cherries into a prepared white cake mix.

Take time to exchange valentines and share together times when you most feel God's love around you. Teachers should share personal experiences of their own, as it is in this way that children come to know how God acts in others' lives and how God can be known to them. Before leaving, share your love and appreciation for each and every person who is in the room and say together Paul's words of love from 1 Corinthians 13:4-7.

CELEBRATING VALENTINE'S DAY IN FAMILY SETTINGS

This is such a fun holiday because sharing love and kindness is a way families are meant to be. It will be easy to get into the spirit of this special day.

As a parent, commit yourself to tell every family member each day in February something special that you LOVE about them. This could indeed become a family project with all members contributing.

Decorate your home with Valentine DECORATIONS (easily found in shopping centers) and include a picture of Jesus as a symbol of the One who shows us best how to love one another.

On or about the first of February, print Bible verses about love on heart SHAPES and place them around the house for family members to read and learn. Then on Valentine's Day each family member can gather up his or her favorite verses and come together for a sharing time. Take note of how many verses have been learned.

Enjoy a special MEAL together. Decorate the table with red and white. A valentine tree makes a good centerpiece and may be made with a tree branch glued onto a block of wood. Hang heart shapes and small valentine cards on the branches.

A heart-shaped meatloaf (your favorite recipe) with ketchup topping will look festive. It may be baked in a heart-shaped pan or formed into a heart by hand.

Finger jello is fun, especially for younger children and can be made by using red jello mixed with half the amount of water called for on the box. Pour it into a pan; when it is set, cut out heart shapes with a cookie cutter. Children can pick them up and eat them.

Enjoy a tossed salad with lettuce, radishes, tomatoes, and bits of apple to give a festive red color. Other vegetables that are family favorites should be part of the meal.

Valentine cut-out cookies are easy to make and together with strawberry ice cream will make a fun dessert.

Butter Cookies

| ½ c. butter | 1 egg |
| ¾ c. sugar | ½ tsp. vanilla |

Beat in electric mixer.

Add:

| 1½ c. flour | ¼ tsp. salt |
| ¼ tsp. baking powder | |

Chill for 1 hour and roll out with a rolling pin onto a floured board. Cut into appropriate shapes with a cookie cutter. Add more flour if the batter appears sticky.

Bake at 375° approximately 8 minutes. Cookies may be decorated with red sugar or frosted.

In our family we like to exchange valentine cards and small gifts at the dinner table. Each family member secretly adds his or her contribution at each place setting. The "gifts" might be as simple as family members writing LOVE LETTERS to each other and sealing them in an envelope.

Have a family together time during dinner. Recall people who are special: family members, neighbors, and church friends. Talk about how each one blesses and enriches your lives. Share a family prayer for them. Then choose a family member or friend who lives away and phone this person together to let the person know how much you care for him/her. A creative way to make your choice would be to write down on pieces of paper (or small hearts) each person you might like to phone and put the pieces into a bowl. Allow the youngest child to draw the name of the "winner" to be called. The remaining names may be drawn once a week until all have received a call. If you find someone is not at home, either choose another name or write that person a family letter.

THE LEGEND OF
ST. VALENTINE

Long ago, in a faraway land, lived a rather ordinary monk named Valentine. He spent much of his day being sad because all his monk brothers were so much smarter than he was. One of them could paint beautiful pictures of Christ; another sang melodic hymns that seemed to reach to the very heavens with praises to God. All the monks had something important to do—either gardening, baking, or weaving fine tapestry.

For a long time only Valentine had no special job. Then one day as he walked through the garden, God spoke to him about love and kindness, and of sharing with others. Valentine became inspired. "I may not have talent," he said, "but anyone can spread love." He developed a plan to write love messages and make love gifts and to deliver them to the villagers. Each day he put together tiny bouquets of flowers and wrote messages on pieces of paper; then afternoons he would wander through the town giving away his treasures.

Soon everyone knew him and loved him, except the king who became very jealous of Valentine's popularity. He ordered Valentine thrown into prison where he was certain all this love and gift giving would end. But even here the happy monk spread love among the guards. Sometimes he would scratch messages on scraps of paper and drop them out the window to the street below where people would gather them up to read.

It wasn't until the king's death that Valentine was finally released from prison and once again was free to spread his words of love throughout the village. When he died, friends declared his birthday should be a special remembrance of him. They called it Valentine's Day and began to send special greetings and cards to loved ones just as Valentine had done.

SHROVE TUESDAY

Shrove comes from the verb "to shrive" which means to confess one's sins and receive absolution, a requirement in the Roman Catholic Church before the solemn beginning of Lent on Ash Wednesday. Shrovetide refers to the three days preceding this time in which people partied and ate up all the fancy foods which were forbidden during the forty days of Lent.

Fat Tuesday, as the day is also called, was named from the custom of eating quantities of meats, eggs, fats and milk. Often pancakes were the meal of the day, for in this way people could consume much of the soon-to-be-forbidden food.

In England a curious game developed among women: they would listen for the church bell to ring, and then grabbing their frying pan with griddle cakes on it, would run for the church, flipping them three times as they hurried down the street. The first woman to arrive received the vicar's blessing. A worship service was soon held, and the bellringers received the pancakes. A church bell rung on this day came to be called the pancake bell.

Among the Pennsylvania Dutch, as well as in Germany, this day is called *Fastnacht* eve. It is the time for consuming doughnuts, a good luck food. These were originally long and thin; but among the Pennsylvania Dutch, the traditional circular doughnut evolved.

Various superstitions accompanied this food, including rubbing the doughnut lard on wounds to assist with healing, on garden tools to protect vegetables from bugs, and on wagon wheels to stop their deterioration or destruction from rats and insects. Failure to eat fastnachts on Shrove Tuesday could cause one an attack of boils, chickens that wouldn't lay eggs, various other maladies, and in general, bad luck.

By far the most celebrative recognition of this holiday occurs in New Orleans where Mardi Gras or Carnival time precedes Lent. The season officially begins on twelfth night or Epiphany and continues until the early morning hours of Ash Wednesday. Parades, fireworks, masked balls, and naming a Carnival king are all a part of the concluding festivities. These are actually a re-creation of the days when New Year's festivals were held at the vernal (spring) equinox. Today Mardi Gras is especially festive in New Orleans, but many Latin American and some European countries celebrate it as well.

Cock fighting used to be a tradition on this day in England, possibly held in remembrance that Peter denied Christ on Good Friday before the cock had crowed three times. Fortunately, this way of celebrating was outlawed in the early 1800s because of its obvious cruelty to animals.

CELEBRATING SHROVE TUESDAY IN CHURCH SETTINGS

An intergenerational evening that begins with a pancake, sausage, and doughnut supper would be a celebration of great traditions for this day. Children in church school classes could make the table decorations and assist in decorating the room in which the party is to be held. Noisemakers and hats such as those suggested for a New Year's party are appropriate to have. Face masks can be made easily on cardboard by outlining children's faces and letting them design the mask. These items may then become centerpieces for the tables. Use crèpe paper streamers on the tables and overhead to give the room a festive appearance.

An older elementary class can assist in making doughnuts.

Doughnuts

1	c. sugar	¼	tsp. cinnamon and nutmeg
2½	tbl. shortening	1	c. milk
3	eggs	4	c. flour
1½	tsp. salt	4	tsp. baking powder

Heat fat (3 to 4 inches) to 375° in deep fryer.

Cream half the sugar with the shortening, beat eggs, add remaining sugar. Mix altogether, then add the dry ingredients (sifted) with milk and a few drops of vanilla. Roll out doughnuts ¼" thick on a floured board. Drop rings into hot fat. Fry about ½ minute on each side or until brown. Remove and drain.

Pancake recipes for making quantities are best obtained with commercial mixes which are quick and simple to prepare. However, if your group is small and you wish to try a more creative pancake, Swedish pancakes are different and delicious.

Swedish Pancakes

1	c. sifted flour	3	eggs
1	tbl. sugar	3	c. milk
½	tsp. salt	4	tbl. melted butter

Beat eggs briskly. Add milk, salt, sugar, and flour, beating slowly. Last add melted butter. Batter will be runny. Fry in grease (bacon fat is best) on a hot grill. Make them large, round, and thin. Fry quickly, allowing them to crisp slightly on the edges. Eat them with butter and powdered sugar, syrup or jelly, or wrapped in fruit and folded together. Peaches, blueberries, or ligonberries (a Swedish berry) are also good.

If guests have come in costume, a parade and the choosing of a King or Queen can follow dinner. Another way to celebrate is to provide circle and line dancing for everyone. The evening might conclude with the singing of many old-fashioned traditional American tunes.

CELEBRATING SHROVE TUESDAY IN FAMILY SETTINGS

A family celebration could include discussing special parties and Mardi Gras which are associated with this day and enjoying a dinner of special foods.

Jambalaya with Ham

1	can condensed cream of mushroom soup	dash of pepper
1¼	c. milk	1 c. cooked green beans
¼	c. chopped onion	1 c. pineapple chunks
¼	tsp. salt	1⅓ c. Minute Rice
		1½ c. diced ham

Combine soup, milk, onion, salt, and pepper together. Mix well. Bring to a boil over medium heat, stirring occasionally. When onions are soft, remove from heat; add Minute Rice and remaining ingredients and put all into a casserole. Top with grated cheese and paprika. Cover and bake at 375° for 20 minutes. Serves 4.

Add a salad with the Jambalaya and serve cake for dessert.

LENT

Ash Wednesday is the day when carnival time is buried and Lent begins. The word *Lent* comes from *lengten,* meaning "when days lengthen," an appropriate word for the spring of the year. It is traditional among Roman Catholics to mark parishioners' foreheads with ashes in the shape of the cross during church services. Palm Sunday greens from the previous year are burned and saved for this purpose. Words of scripture from Genesis 3:20, "You are dust and to dust you shall return," accompany the ritual. Thus one begins a time of penitence and reflection about the meaning of Christ in one's life. This custom is believed to have originated with Pope Gregory around A.D. 600 and was first reserved only for those in need of forgiveness. They would appear barefoot at the front of the altar to do penance for their sins. As family members were often present, it developed into a meaningful experience for them as well and gradually was offered for all members.

Ashes were a sign of penitence in the Old Testament and were accompanied by wearing sackcloth, not bathing, and often sitting among the ashes as Job did (Job 2:8). Early Christian monks sometimes observed this ritual in penitence for their sins and those of others. Today many mainline Protestant churches include ashes as a part of Ash Wednesday worship.

The first observance of Lent was only forty hours in length and was accompanied by strict fasting. Later it was extended to six weeks, or thirty-six days. Sundays are not included, as they are not considered to be days on which to fast because Jesus' resurrection occurred on Sunday, making each one a "little Easter." Finally four more days were added along with Ash Wednesday, making it forty days. This observance always includes periods of denial. For example, certain foods (often meat and sweets) are given up for Lent. Some persons choose to give up parties and other forms of entertainment or even certain attitudes. In England until 1863 there was a law that eggs, meat, and milk not be eaten during this time and those who violated it could be fined or imprisoned. Only the sick and elderly were excused. Fish was the most often eaten food, and money saved was to be given to the poor. Festivities of all kinds, including marriage ceremonies, were strictly forbidden, and theaters were closed as well.

The Lenten cross, a little known ceremony, was used in Roman

28

Catholic families in a worship service and is similar to the Advent wreath ceremony. Originally the Christmas tree was saved until then, when its trunk was cut into the shape of a cross and six or seven candles were placed along it. Among Roman Catholics, the candle in the center of the cross bars was pink and and was lit on the fourth Sunday of Lent, called the "Sunday of the Rose." It was a time to celebrate mothers in England and a joyful moment in the middle of a solemn season. In other traditions, seven candles are used, and the center one is white for Easter and Resurrection. In either ceremony, candles are lit each week and accompanied by Bible reading and prayer.

Spring housecleaning became a custom of Lent (and is also related to Passover). It was a time to remove from the home all the forbidden foods of the season and to clean all cooking utensils in preparation for the holy time. In Passover, it is customary to remove all yeast from the home and bring out special dishes which can only be used at this time.

Special foods not eaten at other seasons of the year came to be part of Lent. In Germany pretzels (usually made only from flour, salt, and water) were made on the Sunday before Lent began and were folded like praying arms. They were never eaten after Palm Sunday.

Hot cross buns, now eaten throughout Lent, were once reserved only for Good Friday. These are believed to have a pagan origin coming from the Egyptians, where small buns stamped with horns were eaten for the worship of Isis, the Mother Goddess. A similar cake was associated with Diana in Greece. The first hot cross buns were similar to Passover bread, flat and containing no yeast. Later they were made of the same dough as the wafer used in communion. Eighteenth-century England popularized them more or less as they appear today with candied fruits inside and crosses on top. It is believed the nursery rhyme, "Hot Cross Buns" ("One-a-penny, two-a-penny hot cross buns, If you have no daughters give them to your sons.") was written because crowds of people purchased their buns from street vendors who barked out the rhyme. Buns were believed to bring good luck to all who ate them. The proceeds were intended for the poor.

Today, as Lent begins, many churches open their sanctuaries for periods of silent prayer, serve communion, or begin a series of Lenten dinners which include music, worship, and study. While most Protestants don't give up foods, it is a time to give an extra offering to the church or a special mission project. Many persons take on difficult projects during this time to reaffirm devotion to Christ and his suffering. Examples include praying for enemies and working for the oppressed.

LENT IN SUNDAY SCHOOL SETTINGS

Many churches offer Lenten programs for adults which may include dinners, special music programs, passion plays, worship, and study. Classes for children may be held as well where it is possible for them to experience a longer learning time, to talk and ask questions, and for teachers to share their own faith. The issues surrounding life and death are puzzling and frequently frightening to children, often leading to misconceptions which they need to express and have explained.

It is also a good opportunity to study who the disciples were and to make puppets of them and to act out stories. Symbols are important illustrations of the faith; learning the meaning of them and making a TREE of symbols related to holy week and Easter is also another good activity. The symbols might be made in a variety of ways: cut out of styrofoam or cardboard, covered with foil or dyed eggshells, then painted or ironed with melted crayon.

Bible verses or prayers can be printed and placed inside plastic eggs, put into small Easter baskets (strawberry baskets work fine), and given to people in hospitals or nursing homes.

Celebrate pretzel Sunday by making and sharing PRETZELS. These were traditionally made on the Sunday before Lent began and eaten throughout the season. Early pretzels were made of flour and water and did not contain leavening. The folded arms represent prayer and the three sections, the trinity. Today, most recipes contain yeast and are no longer eaten only during Lent.

Pretzels

3	c. milk	3	tbl. melted shortening
1	tbl. sugar	7	c. flour
1	package dry yeast		

Heat a small amount of milk until lukewarm, place in warm bowl, and dissolve the yeast packet; add the sugar. Mixture will become foamy after a few minutes. Add the rest of the ingredients and half the flour. Continue to add flour until the dough is fairly firm. On a floured board, knead the mixture by adding a little more flour until the dough is firm. Place in a bowl, cover and set in a warm place to rise, approximately one to one-and-a-half hours.

Take a golfball size piece of dough out of the bowl, re-covering the bowl. With floured hands roll the dough out until it is 14"-16" long. Then form it into pretzel shapes and place pretzels on cookie sheet, keeping them apart as much as possible.

Beaten egg may be brushed on top of each pretzel and coarse salt sprinkled lightly on top. Allow pretzels to rise about 15 minutes longer. Then bake at 400° for 15 minutes or until done. Remove and place on a wire rack to cool. Makes about three dozen.

OBSERVING LENT WITH CHILDREN IN FAMILY SETTINGS

The ancient custom of giving up a favorite food or activity for Lent could become a time for families to eat simpler, perhaps meatless meals several times a week, and use the money that is saved to make a special offering to the church or to a favorite charity.

Meatless Chile Relleno Casserole

1	can (7 oz.) of green chiles	2	tbl. flour
1½	pounds grated cheddar cheese	1	can (11 oz.) evaporated
¾	pound grated jack cheese		milk
4	eggs	1	can (12 oz.) tomato sauce

Rinse and clean chiles, removing the seeds; place half of them in a 9"x 13" casserole. Sprinkle on half of the cheeses, add the remaining chiles, topping with the rest of the cheese. Beat eggs, flour, and milk together and pour this mixture over the cheese and chiles. Bake at 350° for 45 minutes. Add tomato sauce as a topping and bake for 5 minutes longer.

During Lent it is important to participate in ACTIVITIES of the church: Ash Wednesday services, Lenten dinners, study times, as well as special programs offered for children. The ritual of the Lenten cross is included for family observance during evenings at home, Wednesdays, or Sundays after dinner.

As a family, decide to read one of the Gospels all the way through during Lent. Mark is the shortest; and by reading approximately one-third of a chapter each night, it will be possible to do this. Choose a modern translation such as "Good News" (Today's English Version) so that children can better understand it, and then allow time to talk and share questions about the reading.

Plan at least one family home evening and rent a video movie about Jesus' life. There are many available. If local video stores don't have them, contact Ecufilm (1-800-251-8140; Tennessee residents 615-242-6277) for possibilities.

Spring housecleaning is also related to Lent. In keeping with the sacrificial nature of the season, invite children to CLEAN out closets, drawers, and toy boxes, separating out those items no longer needed to give away to an organization or children who can enjoy them.

Hot cross buns are traditional for Lent and can be simple to make when using a packaged roll mix that contains yeast. Mix it according to the directions on the box, add ¾ cup of raisins and two tablespoons of grated orange rind, and allow it to rise in a warm part of the kitchen, following package instructions.

When dough is ready, break off pieces approximately golfball size, roll into a ball, and place in a baking dish (9" x 13"), allowing it to rise a second time. Just before baking, cut a cross on the top of each roll with a knife or scissors. Bake at 375°, 20-25 minutes until browned. Frost with a cross of icing when cooled. Serve for breakfast.

The Lenten Cross

The first Lenten crosses were made from trunks of Christmas trees as a reminder of the joy of Christmas and the sacrifice of Christ on Good Friday. There are at least two variations of its appearance. One is that there be six candles, five purple with a pink one at the joint of the arms (to be lit on the third week of Lent as a sign of hope and thanksgiving). The other tradition uses seven candles: six purple for each Sunday of Lent plus a white one for Easter.

Worship times may begin with Ash Wednesday and be observed each Wednesday thereafter, or they may be held on each Sunday of Lent.

As with Advent wreaths, families might begin a tradition of worship using the Lenten cross. The cross may be purchased (styrofoam is available in the shape of the cross) or made of wood. It should be assembled on Ash Wednesday. At this time the family needs to decide where it should be placed for the Lenten season.

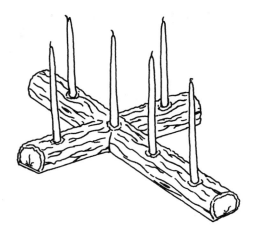

LENTEN CROSS WORSHIP SERVICE

First week of Lent

Reader #1: On Ash Wednesday Lent began. Now is the time of year for us to remember what Jesus means in our lives. Some people wear ashes on their foreheads at the beginning of Lent to remember Jesus' death. Lent will last for forty days just as Jesus spent that length of time in the wilderness.

(Light the first Lenten candle. Read Mark 1:12-13.)

Reader #2: Jesus, like us, was tempted to make wrong choices; but because of his obedience to God, he refused to do this. Instead he chose to serve God in the best way possible.

(Share ways we have made wrong decisions recently, and decide on something to do as a family to show our love to God this Lenten season. Close with a prayer for forgiveness and direction in our lives.)

Second week of Lent

Reader #1: Jesus was the wisest teacher ever known, yet not everyone understood or wanted to follow his teachings.

(Read Luke 4:16-19.)

Reader #2: When Jesus finished these words, he was confronted by the people; some became angry and didn't want to listen to him. They made him leave the city. Sometimes we treat Jesus this way ourselves. We don't listen to or obey Jesus.

(Light the first and second candles. Sing or say together verse one of "Softly and Tenderly Jesus Is Calling." Close with a prayer thanking God for the Bible which tells us about Jesus and for the wise rules for living which he gave us.)

Third week of Lent

Reader #1: Even Jesus' disciples sometimes misunderstood him; one day they argued about which one of them was the greatest.

(Read Luke 9:46-47.)

Reader #2: To Jesus, being the greatest meant being humble like a child; and greatness could also be found in serving others. How can we show service to others this week? Jesus demonstrated this kind of serving to his disciples at the Last Supper.

(Read John 13:4-5. Light three candles. Sing "Dear Master in Whose Life I See." Close with a prayer, asking God to help us find ways to be better Christian servants.)

Fourth week of Lent

Reader #1: Jesus was concerned with empty prayers like those uttered by the Pharisees in public places where they could be noticed. Because of this he taught his followers a new prayer.

(Read Matthew 7:1-14. Discuss the meaning of the words in this prayer. Light four candles.)

Reader #2: Jesus often spent time in prayer himself. On the night he was betrayed he prayed in the Garden of Gethsemane.

(Read Matthew 26:36-39. Close with the Lord's Prayer, sung or said.)

Fifth week of Lent

Reader #1: Parables are short stories with important messages. Jesus told many such stories; one of them is called the prodigal son.

(Read Luke 15:11-24.)

Reader #2: God forgives those who do wrong, just as the father in the story forgave his son.

(Light five candles.)

Reader #2: Jesus even asked God's forgiveness of those persons who were responsible for his death.

(Read Luke 23:34. Sing "Tell Me the Stories of Jesus" and close with a prayer that we learn to be more loving and forgiving of others who wrong us.)

Sixth week of Lent

Reader #1: Before his death, Jesus desired to celebrate one last supper with his followers so that they would better remember him.

(Read Matthew 26:26-29. Talk about the meaning of the Last Supper and the communion service which is the way we remember this event. Light all six candles and share a communion ritual of bread and grape juice together as you recall the lessons learned and scripture verses of the past six weeks.)

Reader #2: Jesus' message to us is about loving others, helping persons in need.

(Read John 21:15-18. Close with a promise to be better disciples and followers of Jesus.)

St. Patrick's Day

The story of Patrick of Ireland is a legend. No one is even certain whether March 17 celebrates his birth or his death, but most people believe it is the latter. Legend is so intertwined with possible facts that many historians have come to believe that there were two and perhaps more St. Patricks whose stories are combined.

The place of his birth is also uncertain, although it is generally agreed that he was born about A.D. 386 in the village of Nemphthur and his father was a town councilor. (Another tale makes him a native of Tours in France.)

At the age of sixteen, he, along with many other people, was carried away by pirates to northern Ireland and sold into slavery. It is known he became a Christian evangelist there and also a bishop, but scholars doubt that this is the same Patrick who visited and Christianized Scotland and the Isle of Man.

It is believed that after six years of slavery, acting upon a dream in which he was told to escape, he fled to the harbor, boarded a ship, and returned to England. His captivity had heightened his religious conscience and turned him to God and the priesthood. He did travel to Gaul, then part of Italy, where he studied in various monasteries, but eventually returned to Ireland in an effort to win converts. This was a land of Druidic religious beliefs, and he met with considerable opposition which resulted in arrest and imprisonment.

Among his feats was to change a Druidic pagan fire-fighting ritual into an Easter Christian ceremony by lighting his own fires on hillsides and declaring Jesus as the light of the world.

It is said he plucked a shamrock to convey to the king and others the trinitarian concept of God; thus this symbol, along with cross, harp, and baptismal font (since he won so many converts), came to be associated with him.

The story of his driving snakes and other vermin from Ireland is probably fanciful, yet various tales are told of how he accomplished this. One story relates that he beat on a drum as he preached, until one day his drum broke on the way to a worship service. An angel appeared and repaired it just as a large snake appeared. He went on to preach; and when he finished the sermon, all snakes suddenly vanished. In another legend he is said to have vanquished all snakes but one, which he tricked into entering a box though the snake said it was too small. "Show me," Patrick said, whereupon the animal crawled in and Patrick snapped the lid shut.

Although St. Patrick's Day is popular in Ireland, it is an even bigger day in parts of the United States. It is heralded by a parade in New York City and other places, along with lively parties and wearing of the green. Touches of St. Patrick may be seen across the United States on this day in hats, ties, boutonnieres, and other apparel. Even foods and drinks are often colored for the occasion, and some people have been known to tint their hair green for the day. Shamrock plants are often sold in nurseries and grocery stores.

In schools even non-Irish children will wear green so as not to be pinched by others. Special foods of the day include Irish stew, "Irish" baked potatoes, and generally anything green in color.

CELEBRATING ST. PATRICK'S DAY
IN SUNDAY SCHOOL SETTINGS

Play Irish tunes as children are arriving in class. Let those who come early make green icing, frost cupcakes, and prepare lemonade or another drink for the class snack.

When everyone is there, teach a St. Patrick's Day song, then ask children to help you name some characteristics of a "Good Christian." List their answers on the board or on newsprint. Then together share names of some people who fit the description they've just written; these may be historical figures, people today, those in our congregation, and those known to the world.

When this is completed tell them about Patrick, a special Christian who lived a long time ago. Use the shamrock to share the concept of God as Creator, Son, and Holy Spirit as Patrick did with his people.

Share some of the problems which exist in Ireland today between Catholics and Protestants and how important it is to develop cooperation and compromise, not conflict between differing groups.

Conflict and Cooperation

Needed: One set of blocks of varying sizes and shapes (may be purchased from a toy store).

Children may sit in a circle with the blocks in the center.

Instructions: Each child needs to help build a structure by putting one block on top of another until all the blocks have been used. The first time it should be a game of competition. As each child chooses a block and places it on top of the others, he or she tries to make it as difficult as possible for the next player to succeed without causing all the blocks to tumble.

Once they have fallen, talk about times when we move ahead without consulting others or are selfish and concerned only with our own winning. Say that this hurts others as well as whatever we are building around us.

Now play the game with new rules. No one wins unless all the blocks are used without any of them tumbling. Again one child at a time must choose and place a block in order to build the structure. They may, however, ask for advice from the class before choosing. This time discuss the need for everyone to care about others in order to build successfully. This care is true in families, in work, and in play.

Other class activities might include:

1. Writing prayers which stress love and cooperation.
2. Making tray favors for a nursing home.
   To make, cut out shamrock shapes, glue them onto a lace doily and attach a small nut cup in the center of the shamrock.

3. Make leprechauns using toilet paper rolls and green felt. Instructions included.

Class time should conclude with REFRESHMENTS prepared ahead, the teacher sharing a leprechaun LEGEND from a library book, and prayers which the children have written.

One alternate class activity would be to visit a Roman Catholic church, talk with a priest about Catholics and Protestants, and participate in a worship service there.

Directions for Making a Leprechaun

Glue green felt body, gold belt, and pointed collar on to a toilet paper roll. Fold each leg in half lengthwise and place a wire inside, allowing it to project out at one end approximately ½" to attach to the foot. This will allow the legs and feet to bend. Staple each leg to the back side of the toilet paper roll. Cut out four pieces of felt for the feet, and glue two to each foot, one on either side of the wire.

Form the arms much the same way, except make the wire 1" longer than the arms, so this can be punched through the felt and inside the toilet paper roll to hold it firm.

A 1⅝" piece of styrofoam will form the face. Add eyes, nose, and mouth to it. Fold the green hat into a cone until it makes a small enough cone to fit the head. Staple the hat pieces to hold them, and use straight pins to attach the hat to the head.

Leprechaun Pattern

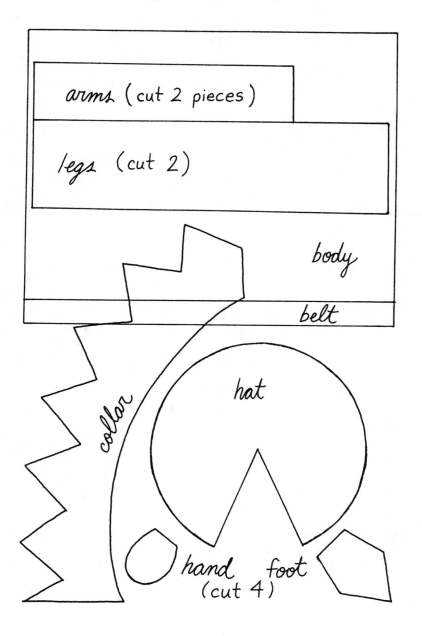

CELEBRATING ST. PATRICK'S DAY IN HOMES

This holiday is a fun one whether or not you are Irish. Prepare a DINNER of special foods: shamrock salad, Irish stew, and lime dessert, or baked "Irish" potatoes stuffed with elaborate toppings (sour cream, mushrooms, creamed vegetables, grated cheese, or bacon).

For a festive table setting, choose green napkins and streamers, shamrocks (real or paper), and balloons in which you have placed a special Irish blessing. These may be attached to each person's chair. Blessings may include: 1. Have a good day always and in all ways. 2. May the blessings of each day be the blessing you need most. 3. May the saddest day in your future be no worse than the happiest day of your past. 4. May the sun always shine on your windowpane. May a rainbow be certain to follow each rain. 5. May the hand of a friend always be near you. 6. May God fill your heart with gladness to cheer you. 7. May you have all happiness and luck that life can hold, and at the end of all your rainbows may you find a pot of gold.

During dinner, talk about Christians, such as Patrick, who left such an impact on the lives of those around them that centuries later they are still remembered with special celebrations. Break your balloons to find your special blessing.

Irish Stew

1	lb. chopped lamb	1	tsp. salt
1	onion		dash of pepper
4	chopped potatoes	2	tbl. flour
4	chopped carrots and parsnips	1	c. water

Brown lamb in frying pan, add vegetables, mix flour with water and cook in a slow cooker on low heat for five hours.

Lime Delight Dessert

Prepare crust first:
2   c. chocolate wafers (Oreos are okay.)
½   c. melted butter
Mix together and press into 9″ x 11″ pan.

Filling:
1   large pkg. lime jello
2   c. water (hot)
¾   c. sugar

Mix these ingredients together. Add ⅔ cup lime juice concentrate, 3 tsp. lemon juice. Allow to cool and stir in one small container of whipping cream, whipped. Pour mixture into the crust and chill.

APRIL FOOL'S DAY

Many years ago New Year's celebrations were held in the spring since this is the time of new life and new beginnings. When our calendar changed to the present one, some persons were reluctant to give up their holiday and were greatly teased by friends who would send them gag gifts and notes with "April Fool" written on them. It later became customary to send friends on nonsensical errands labeled "sleeveless errands." These were especially popular in England where people would go to grocery stores for "pigeon milk," the library for a book on the "history of Eve's mother," or to a meeting that didn't exist. Often elaborate notes sent through the mail would describe a meeting location at a place where there wasn't even a building.

An explanation for the custom of practical jokes revolves around the trial of Jesus as he was sent from Annas to Caiaphas to Pilate to Herod and back to Pilate in a kind of meaningless trial. (See John 18:12-40 and 19:1-15.) The story of Noah and the Ark has also been associated with this day when it is said Noah mistakenly sent the dove out to find land on the first of the month (generally associated with April, see Genesis 8:6-13); in retaliation people are sent on hapless errands. However, neither of these explanations is taken seriously.

A tale is told of the wise fools of Gotham who prevented the King of England from invading their town by behaving like fools. Any territory through which the king passed automatically became a part of his realm. However, townspeople set up a road block at the entrance gates; and when messengers wandered inside, what they saw astounded them as men were rolling cheeses down the street to market, drowning eels in pools, and busily capturing a cuckoo bird and the tree in which it sat. Believing everyone in that town to be crazy, the king turned in another direction.

Much more ancient civilizations have their claim on April first. The day was associated with Roman and Greek mythology when the festivals of Venus and Roman Saturnalia were held. Saturnalia involved a medieval feast of fools.

April has been a somewhat fateful month in United States history, since the Revolutionary War (battles of Lexington and Concord) began then, as did the Civil War with the firing on Ft. Sumter. The

Spanish American War and the declaration of war against Germany for World War 1 additionally have April dates.

This is a holiday of special delight to children, for the playing of tricks on one another and on adults (when they can get away with it) sends them into gales of laughter. Pinning "kick me" and other signs on friends' backs, gluing a coin to the sidewalk, telling people their clothes are torn, faces are dirty, or a bug is on their shoulder and then shouting, "April fool!" is considered hilarious fun on the part of the trickster. All in all it's a day to enjoy a bit of laughter, time for joke telling, and harmless tricks in which no one gets hurt.

APRIL FOOL'S DAY
IN SUNDAY SCHOOL SETTINGS

Since this is a day with no religious significance, it can be a time for parents and children to come to church and enjoy a class supper with some entertainment. Guests might be invited to come dressed as clowns, wearing mismatched clothing (two different colored socks and shoes), or clothing could be worn backwards. Children and parents might reverse roles, each wearing clothing styles the other would ordinarily wear.

Play an opening get-acquainted GAME called "Crossed Signals." Each person chooses an instruction card and tries to follow it completely before the person with the opposite instructions can undo it. Instructions may include the following ideas:

1. Move all the chairs around the tables.
2. Move all the chairs against the wall.
3. Collect all the plates and put them on the counter.
4. Fold all the napkins and put them at each person's plate.
5. Set the table with the plates at each setting.
6. Unfold the napkins and take them to the kitchen.

It will be more fun if ideas which best fit your own situation are chosen; so use your imagination and have fun with the game. Recognize anyone who is able to complete a chore before it is undone.

About ten minutes before dinner, hand out the MYSTERY MENU (on piece of typing paper folded in half) which has been typed or written for each person to fill out and return to the servers.

Page 1.

1. Today you will be served a 4-course meal. You are allowed 4 items per course. Study the menu carefully before choosing. Do not compare your choices with anyone else.

2. Please indicate by numbers in the space below which items you desire for each course. Choices are important because eating utensils are included in the hidden words. At the end of each course all items, including silverware, will be collected before the next course begins.

3. In five minutes the menus will be collected. Please put your name at the top of the page.

Course Selection

1st	2nd	3rd	4th
___	___	___	___
___	___	___	___
___	___	___	___
___	___	___	___

- -

Page 2.

Menu

Please list the menu in two long columns filling the paper.

1. Grapes of Wrath, 2. Chip off the old block, 3. Crystal clear, 4. It takes two, 5. Blood and guts, 6. I wanta pop, 7. London fog, 8. Yellow snow, 9. Stick it where you will, 10. Nothin' like loving, 11. It's a trap, 12. Slice of life, 13. Fun to get dirty, 14. Flying ace, 15. Farmer in the dell, 16, Soft 'n' sticky.

Page 3

Notice

1. Emily Post rules of etiquette do not apply.
2. We offer leftovers if anything is left over.
3. Anyone leaving anything on his or her plate will do the dishes.

The Management

Answers to menu code (known only to the cook and servers):
1. grape juice, 2. toothpick, 3. water, 4. chopsticks, 5. spaghetti or lasagna, 6. popcorn, 7. soup, 8. lemon jello with marshmallows, 9. bread stick, 10. Oreo cookie, 11. fork, 12. knife, 13. napkin, 14. spoon, 15. salad, 16. garlic bread.

The meal menu might also be prepared in a foreign language, one that only the preparer knows. Here's one in Swedish:
1. ärter (peas), 2. sallad (slice of lettuce), 3. kniv (knife), 4. sked (spoon), 5. mös (mashed potatoes), 6. morötter (carrots), 7. Kottbullar (meatballs), 8 gaffel (fork), 9. glass (ice cream), 10. smö kaka (cookie), 11. saft (soft drink), 12. applesin (orange juice), 13. päron (slice of pear), 14. ost (cheese), 15. servett (napkin), 16. sås (gravy)

The after-dinner entertainment might include a clown, mime, or a magician. However, this might also be an opportunity to invite children to sing the songs they have been learning in class and also a time to share any plays or videotapes or other special learning that has taken place.

One further idea for an April Fool's Day party could be a MYSTERY RIDE. Each driver receives a clue which children and driver must decipher together. They drive to that location where a second clue will be waiting. This will continue until they have gone to four or five different locations. Finally they should arrive at their destination, which could be a pizza parlor, ice cream store, or home of one of the children where a dinner or party is waiting. An emergency phone number should be given to each driver in a sealed envelope to be opened only if they become hopelessly lost. In a party of this type most of the fun is found in trying to get to the destination.

APRIL FOOL'S DAY IN FAMILY SETTINGS

Although children enjoy this day as an opportunity for joke playing, there are better ways to celebrate it. A TOPSY TURVY day is one idea to try. This may be done by serving dinner at breakfast; burger patty or steak, with potatoes (fried), and fruit. Then for dinner serve pancakes or another breakfast meal.

Should this idea not be appealing, try serving dinner in reverse order, beginning with dessert and ending with salad. An upside-down cake would make an appropriate dessert.

Fruit Upside-Down Cake

One package cake mix (white or yellow). Mix it according to directions. Arrange slices of fruit, (peaches, apricots, or pineapple) on the bottom of a 9" x 13" pan. Mix ¾ cup melted margarine with 1½ cups packed brown sugar. Spread this mixture around the fruit. Add the cake mix and bake at 350° until done. When cake is done, serve it warm with whipped cream.

Plan a children's party, inviting each child to bring a favorite riddle or joke. Give a prize to the child with the best one.

GAMES may include a scavenger hunt with children in pairs searching for a variety of items from neighbors, such as piece of soap, paper clip, band aid, button, rubber band, used envelope, and napkin.

Another game can be to unscramble names or words which would finally make a sentence. Once deciphered, the message would direct a child to a specific location where a prize or second coded message awaits.

Preschool Puzzle Game

Items needed: 1 preschool puzzle for every participant. Children will divide into two teams of equal size and sit in circles on the floor with a puzzle in a box in front of each of them. At a given signal, an adult dumps all puzzle pieces into the center of the circle and scrambles them, giving each child an equal number of pieces.

Game Rules

1. No one may talk or make sounds once the game begins.
2. All players must attempt to put their own puzzle together with the pieces they have.
3. Players may give pieces away to others but may not ask anyone for anything.
4. As each player completes his or her own puzzle, he/she may help another player, but again no talking or taking puzzle pieces from another player is allowed.

The team which learns cooperation most quickly will win the game. A discussion of the benefits of learning to work together is appropriate with this game.

Since springtime is fresh and new, serve:

Flowerpot Sandwiches

Items needed:

3 slices of bread per child trimmed into circles of three different sizes

Place the smallest slice on the bottom, fill with desired sandwich filling (peanut butter & jelly, egg salad, etc.). Place the second smallest circle of bread on top and add a second (preferably different) filling. Place the largest circle of bread on the top.

A cherry tomato, radish trimmed like a flower, or circle of raw carrot will make a flower. These may be speared with a wooden skewer such as the kind used for shish kebab and stuck into the flowerpot. A sprig of mint, parsley, or celery leaf will make the leaves.

An interesting ice cream cup dessert can be made by melting chocolate chips and pouring them into paper baking cups which have been placed in muffin tins. Be sure to cover sides and bottom with chocolate, forming a cup. Refrigerate to harden. Remove paper carefully from the cups when the chocolate is firm and fill with vanilla ice cream.

PALM SUNDAY AND
HOLY WEEK

MARCH-APRIL

The Gospels (Matthew 21:8-9, Mark 11:1-10, and Luke 19:28-40) tell the story of Jesus' procession into Jerusalem several days before the beginning of Passover. This event marks the first Palm Sunday and the beginning of Holy Week. It is believed that the actual observance of this day began with Bishop Cyril in Jerusalem during the latter part of the fourth century. The day began with a procession in which children were carried into the city on their parents' shoulders while waving branches of palms and olive leaves. Many years later, probably during the twelfth century, the day was recognized in Rome as a Christian holiday.

The Old Testament records occasions when processions with palm branches occurred to honor kings and other special people. Second Kings 9:13 records a procession to honor Jehu as king. Zechariah 9:9 refers to a procession with palm branches, The text is used in the New Testament as a prophecy referring to Jesus. In the Apocrypha, 1 Maccabees 13:51, another celebration is recorded in honor of Simon, following the cleaning of the temple.

Superstitions arose regarding palm leaves. Perhaps they protected against evil. Maybe they could charm away lightning storms. In many parts of the world palm fronds are not available; so olive, willow, and other leafy branches are substituted. This led to renaming the day Branch Sunday in England and Blossom Sunday in Germany. Processions in which a priest rides a donkey and people carpet the walkway with branches, leaves, and clothing have been reenacted on this day.

In Rome, palms are blessed in the Sistine Chapel; and numerous Christians gather to watch the procession of the Pope seated in St. Peter's chair and carried on the shoulders of eight men.

The story of Jesus overturning the tables in the temple, and thus cleansing it, is generally associated with Monday of Holy Week; although as told in Matthew 22:15-21 and Mark 11:11-12, this event appears to have occurred immediately following the Palm Sunday procession.

Tuesday is the day to remember the Pharisees who attempted to trap Jesus into making a blasphemous statement (Matthew 22:15-21). This is also the day when Jesus predicted the destruction of the temple.

Spy Wednesday is the name given to the next day, when it is

believed that Judas Iscariot met with the priests to betray Jesus and accept his thirty pieces of silver.

Maundy Thursday is the day on which Jesus and his disciples celebrated the Passover or Last Supper, though today we would expect Passover on Friday. This story, along with the footwashing, may be found in Matthew 26:17-29 and John 13:1-17.

Maundy Thursday

The word *Maundy* comes from a Latin word *mandatum*, meaning commandment. On this day is celebrated "a new commandment which I give to you, that you love one another" (John 13:34-35). During the Middle Ages, people developed the custom of washing the feet of the poor and giving them gifts. King Edward III of England reportedly did this.

Some churches have worship services called Tennebrae services in which candles are extinguished, altars stripped and washed, and communion served. These have also been held on Wednesday and Friday of Holy Week. A loud clap like thunder sometimes sounds to recall the scripture in Matthew 27:50-52, when at the time of Jesus' death an earthquake occurred, the rocks split, and the curtain of the temple was torn in half. Services on Maundy Thursday might also include sacrificial meals and footwashing or handwashing ceremonies.

Good Friday

This day commemorating the death of Christ is a time of mourning throughout Christianity. Some churches drape the altar and cross in black and extinguish all light. Why we call it "good" is something of a mystery. Perhaps "good" refers to the gift of God's salvation found in the death and resurrection of Christ, but others suggest that it was really meant to be God's Friday. Older names given to this day are Long Friday, the Festival of the Crucifixion, and Day of Salvation.

An early ritual of Good Friday, called the "Veneration of the Cross," involved a bishop seated on a chair near a linen cloth-covered table. Upon the table was placed a casket in which was carried a wooden cross. Bishop and deacons guarded the wood as the congregation came one by one to kiss the cross.

Three-hour worship services beginning at noon are also traditional today and often are ecumenical in nature. The theme of worship is usually based on the seven last words of Jesus (Luke 23:34, 23:43, 23:46; John 19:26-27, 19:28, 19:30; and Mark 15:34). These services are often shortened to fifteen-minute segments, allowing working people the opportunity to worship during lunch hour.

One interesting legend involves the dogwood tree, because some storytellers believe that it was this tree that was used to make the cross for the crucifixion. We are told that the dogwood is not very tall because it suffered so much that the risen Christ ordered it shortened forever with its flowers forming a cross, rust-colored nail marks on each petal, a red stain in the center, and a crown of thorns surrounding it so all will remember the crucifixion.

Holy Saturday

Like Good Friday this became a day of remembrance in the fourth century. At first it was a day for baptism and first communion of new converts, wearing new, white linen clothes for this experience. It later became traditional with Easter and putting on a new life in Christ. Worship services referred to Matthew 27:62-66 and the guarding of the tomb by soldiers to prevent Christ's escape and fulfillment of the resurrection.

Today it is primarily observed by Roman Catholic and Orthodox churches. One ceremony celebrated by them is the blessing of the Paschal candle which is placed on the altar and left there until Ascension Day. Five grains of incense are sprinkled in remembrance of burial spices and the five wounds in Jesus' side. In Los Angeles on Olvera Street, it is the day for the blessing of the animals by a priest. In Mexico, there developed a custom of staging a Passion Play during each night of Holy Week with Saturday's story devoted to Judas. A papier mâché figure representing him is stuffed and ignited. Firecrackers inside the figure cause it to burst.

This is also the day to dye Easter eggs and prepare the special breads traditional in some countries.

EASTER

This is unquestionably the most important day in the Christian calendar. It is a time of joy, excitement, and crowded houses of worship. Sanctuaries are brightly decorated with lilies and other spring flowers. Choirs, at their best, are often enhanced with musical instruments. The number and times of services are altered to accommodate larger attendances, and pancake breakfasts are common in many churches.

The resurrection accounts of Jesus' life are found in Matthew 28, Mark 16, Luke 24, and John 20 and 21, and in the writings of Paul. Early Christians named a new day of worship in order to celebrate this event weekly, referring to Sunday as "little Easter."

While each Gospel writer differs somewhat in his interpretation of the resurrection, leaving many unanswered questions, it is most certain that the disciples experienced something beyond the ordinary that caused them to change from frightened, unhappy men into the fearless leaders of the faith which they became.

There was great division over the date for Easter, some believing it should always be on a Sunday. Among Eastern Orthodox Christians, there was the additional belief that it should follow Passover. The Council of Nicaea in 325 decided on the first Sunday after the first full moon after the vernal equinox (March 21—the date when day and night are of equal length). It may be as early as March 22 or as late as April 25. Though this scheduling seems unduly complicated, it was decided upon so early Christians would have a full moon by which to travel on Easter pilgrimages. Orthodox churches continue to schedule Easter following Passover and seldom celebrate it the same day as other Christians.

Easter was named after the Anglo-Saxon goddess Eostre whose holiday fell at the vernal equinox. She heralded the beginning of spring and the return of fertility. In some countries the day was first called Pascha in remembrance of Passover. Early celebrations lasted eight days; it was a time for happy crowd gathering, no work, giving to the poor, freeing slaves, and joyous eating and partying.

For a number of years European countries named an Easter king, dressing him in royal robes and crown and parading him around the streets. Long ago no fires could be lit on Easter eve, and in Finland it was feared wolves would attack cattle if they saw fire. In great secrecy,

51

the Easter celebration was prepared lest witches discover them and spoil the day. Pastors blessed all grain and foods and handed out to parishioners lamb symbols carved in wax. Later the symbols were made of wood and worn as necklace charms.

Eastern Orthodox churches have colorful and moving celebrations on this day with candlelighting ceremonies held throughout the world. Services are held in the middle of the night, sanctuaries are darkened, and the priest appears in an elaborately decorated robe with a lighted taper. From this the congregation receives the "light of Christ" until the splendor of many candles surrounds everyone. In some countries people try to carry the light home to relight the family fire for a new beginning.

The somber Puritans curtailed Easter celebrations in the American colonies; but Roman Catholic, Anglican, and Lutheran immigrants introduced their traditions to the people. Moravian Christians in Pennsylvania brought with them the celebration of the love feast: Saturday afternoon worship with trombone choir and also midnight worship followed by house-to-house singing until dawn. Breakfast of coffee and sugar-cake and a walk to the cemetery to face the rising sun concluded the joyful time.

Many customs from pagan celebrations have adapted well to Christian recognition of this day. Eostre's fertility symbols were eggs and rabbits. Eggs have been symbolic throughout the world and are also used with Passover. Dying eggs and painting them elaborately is a tradition in many lands. They are also hidden for children to find and used in games such as eggrolling contests (White House lawn), egg tapping (trying to break another's egg without breaking your own), and egg tossing games. Eggrolling is considered symbolic of the rolling away of the large rock from Christ's tomb.

In Germany, the Easter hare was believed to hide eggs in homes of good children. Parents spent the evening before Easter painting and hiding the eggs, while children nervously wondered if they had been good enough for the hare to visit them. Since Easter is connected with the full moon, and the hare is a nocturnal animal, he was considered the one who "opened Spring." The hare has since been replaced by the rabbit as the symbol.

Ancient people believed that lion cubs were born dead and resurrected after three days, making this animal and the butterfly (which is resurrected from the tomb of the crysallis) other symbols of Easter.

Flowers, a symbol of spring and new life, are also part of this day. The Bermuda lily, treasured for its white color and pleasant fragrance, resembles a trumpet, which is the instrument often used to herald the resurrection.

Sunrise services probably have their origin in the sunrise discovery of the empty tomb (Luke 24:1) but also relate back to the vernal equinox and welcoming the return of the sun, now changed to be the Son of Man.

Easter Monday is a holiday in some countries of Europe where only a minimum of work is done and celebrations continue with parades and partying. Easter Monday is also observed as a holiday in some places in the U.S.A.

PALM SUNDAY, LENT, AND EASTER IN SUNDAY SCHOOL SETTINGS

Invite children to participate in worship on Palm Sunday by being part of a special PROCESSION into the sanctuary. They can wear biblical costumes and sandals and wave palms or other leafy branches. Paper ones can be substituted if real ones are unobtainable. Choose a representative of Jesus to walk in the midst of them, preferably a man with a beard, in costume. They will move to background music, walk down the aisle to the altar, and stand facing it. "Jesus" will face the cross with arms outstretched, then, before the music ends, lead the children out of the sanctuary. A rehearsal time is needed if this is to be a meaningful experience. Boys and girls can then make palm crosses and present them to members of the congregation at the close of worship.

To make Palm Crosses: Fold a sheet of green construction paper in half lengthwise—12" x 16" is a good size to use. Draw and cut out an oval like-leaf and cut out the individual fronds with scissors as shown in the illustration on the following page.

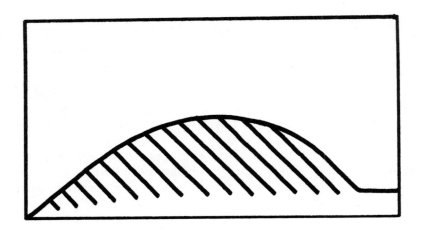

In many parts of the United States, school vacation coincides with Holy Week. If this is the case for you, plan for a SPRING VACATION SCHOOL of anywhere from one to four days. Separate classes are needed for younger children; however, those third grade and older may be grouped together in a learning center setting.

Begin each session by singing songs and hymns related to Lent and Easter. "Tell Me the Stories of Jesus" and "Christ the Lord Is Risen Today" are two important choices. Class time should include a study period for learning the events of Jesus' life from Palm Sunday to Easter. This may be done through Bible reading, storytelling, films, and videos. Follow this by painting murals depicting what Jesus did each day of Holy Week, participating in a role play of many of the day's events, and studying the important symbols of this season.

This season of the year is also a good time for teachers to talk to children about death and to allow them to ask questions. This can be helpful in clearing up misconceptions which children may have. Many good books are available to assist teachers with this. Since spring HOUSECLEANING is traditional in homes, children might enjoy fixing up the sanctuary by sharpening pew pencils, cleaning marks off backs of pews, straightening up hymnal racks, and putting in a fresh supply of visitor cards and other leaflets.

If your church is one which hosts a pancake BREAKFAST on Easter, children might make decorations for the tables. For an Easter symbol tree, use a tree branch set in a block of wood and covered with paper symbols and egg-shaped decorations. Cover half an eggshell with fabric or paint, and glue a piece of ribbon around it as a hanger. A piece of cotton may be glued inside and a small bunny or chick attached to it. The shell might also be filled with dirt and planted with grass seed. By watering it, grass will sprout in a few days and be quite attractive on the tree. Plastic eggs might also be used for this activity.

Paper Easter lily bouquets (pattern included) can also make attractive table DECORATIONS.

Easter Lily Pattern

Fold white lily into a cone with the half moon as the center. Match A to the back side of B, matching it up to the line on the pattern. Attach 3 stamens to the top of the green stem folded in half—insert it through the opening at the bottom of the lily and staple together.

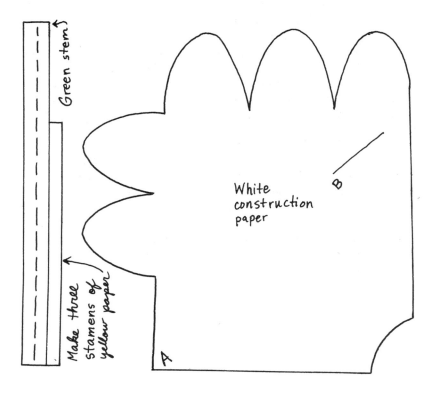

For other activities children can make hospital tray FAVORS by using a paper egg carton and trimming it to form a bunny face. This favor also serves as an attractive egg cup for Easter morning. Empty eggshells can be used to make candles. Place a small piece of wick inside and pour melted paraffin or candle wax into it. (Crayon shavings added will dye the wax.) When it hardens, peel off the shell to create an Easter candle.

Greeting CARDS are easy to make using dyed eggshell pieces to fill in a variety of designs from eggs and rabbits to crosses or flowers. Food color, water, and a drop of vinegar makes as good a dye as any which can be purchased. A card (or small gift PLAQUE) can be made with pieces of felt forming a vase of flowers. Small buttons glued into the centers are attractive, and they can also be used to decorate the vase.

In many churches Easter is a day when Sunday school classes are not held. Yet the message of this day is an important one for children. So the last day of Spring Vacation School may be another time to learn about Easter. Create a large mural (floor to ceiling) of the empty tomb, rock rolled away, with perhaps blue sky above and a floor-to-ceiling tree. Plan a play which is a TV news INTERVIEW outside the tomb. Children might each write their own parts after studying the resurrection story. They should pretend to be curiosity seekers (amidst a few followers of Jesus). The "reporter" holding a microphone would then ask each one what happened here. Answers would range from "I don't know," to "Jesus was buried here and now he's missing," or "I don't know who Jesus is. Will someone tell me?" and "He has risen, I have seen and talked to him." This play should be videotaped. Children love the instant replay it provides.

On this last day of Spring Vacation School, each child should bring several hardboiled eggs to dye in class. Each one can decorate an Easter basket and participate in an egg hunt around the church buildings or grounds. A special Easter worship time would conclude the school's events.

Easter Greeting Card

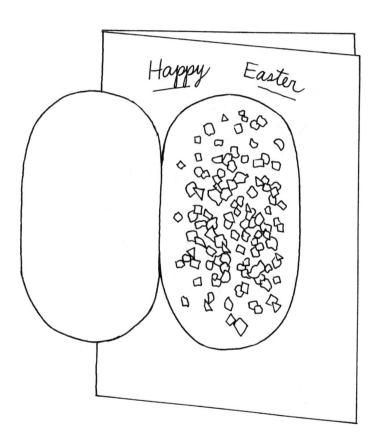

Easter Card or Plaque to Hang

Needed: 5" x 7" piece of wood, 5 small buttons for the vase plus a button for each flower and different colors of felt for vase, stems, and flowers. (Of course, children may create their own flower and vase designs.)

PALM SUNDAY, HOLY WEEK TO EASTER
IN FAMILY SETTINGS

Palm Sunday is a happy day in the midst of a more somber season. There is opportunity here to list together what qualities make a person great or important, to share why people praised Jesus on this day (and deserted him so soon after), and to read the Palm Sunday story to children.

On each day of Holy Week, share the events of that day with children. Help them to put the story in chronological order, but be careful to allow time for questions as you do this.

Attend Holy Week worship services in your own church or a neighborhood church. Communion is usually celebrated at Maundy Thursday WORSHIP and provides an opportunity to explain this ritual to children, by allowing them to participate. Good Friday services are often ecumenical in nature and are sometimes held from noon to 3:00 P.M., with pastors from several denominations taking part.

Scandinavian people have a custom surrounding spring which is appropriate here. They cut tree branches when the buds are almost ready to burst open, put them in water, and decorate them with brightly colored pieces of tissue paper. Pinch 2 inch squares in the middle to form a flower; attach a very thin wire to the pinched-off portion and wire them to the branches. These twigs at first appear dead, but the tissue flowers brighten them. Finally, when the leaves appear, there is the symbol of new life or resurrection. Depending on when spring comes in your part of the country, and how early Easter is, this activity might come during or even after Lent.

Dying Easter eggs, making baskets, and baking Easter bread are activities children will delight in sharing.

This year make a basket or box of goodies to give away. Instead of candies, substitute fresh fruit and canned foods, including a ham. The children can decorate the outside of the box with bright contact paper and paper egg shapes. Easter grass placed around the foods can add to the festiveness. An offering to a needy family might also be made this year instead of purchasing new Easter clothing.

Easter Bread: Prepare your favorite bread recipe or purchase dough which only needs to rise. When ready to bake, add 3 or 4 hard-boiled eggs (in the shell) which have been dyed pretty colors and bake according to directions. (It isn't necessary to buy egg dyes—food color and water will dye just as well.) Cut in slices big enough to include the egg.

Moravian Love Feast Buns

1 package yeast	1 tsp. salt
¼ c. tepid water	¼ tsp. warm mashed potatoes
1 c. sugar	7-8 c. flour
1 egg, beaten	2 c. lukewarm water
¼ c. soft butter	Melted butter for glazing

Dissolve yeast in ¼ cup tepid water; add sugar to beaten egg. Then add softened butter, salt, potatoes (warm), and yeast mixture. Add flour and warm water alternately, to make a soft but firm dough. On lightly floured board or in hands knead until smooth. Cover with warm cloth and set it in a warm place to rise. When dough doubles in size, punch it down and make into buns 3" to 4" in diameter. Place on cookie sheet and bake in 400° oven about 20 minutes. Brush with melted butter. Makes 18-20 buns.

Making chocolate Easter eggs is fun and quite easy to do.

Chocolate Easter Eggs

2 lb. confectioners sugar	maraschino cherries, drained and
¼ lb. butter or oleo	chopped
1 tsp. vanilla	coconut
1 can condensed milk	peanut butter
	1 large pkge. choc. chips

Mix the ingredients together. Separate dough into three sections; if too moist, add more sugar. Into one section add drained, chopped maraschino cherries. Into the second section add chopped coconut, and into the third a large spoonful of peanut butter. (Nuts, food coloring, extracts, and cocoa can create other flavors.) Roll these into egg shapes and refrigerate to harden each one.
Prepare a coating by melting one large package of chocolate chips. Dip each egg into this, covering it completely. Then place it on waxed paper and refrigerate to harden and set the chocolate. A small amount of paraffin (1 tbl.) may be melted if the chocolate isn't setting properly.

Easter Basket Cake

This is simple to make. Any flavor cake mix may be used, mixed according to directions, and baked in two 9" round cake pans.
When done, remove a center circle from the top layer, put the two layers together with jam or icing. Frost the top and sides of the cake, covering around the center circle but not inside.
Dye 1 cup of coconut with green food color that has been mixed in water (approximately ¾ cup of water and 4 drops of dye). Dry the coconut on paper

towels, then place it in the center of the cake. Add jellybeans and other Easter candy, and cookie sprinkles. To finish the cake, pipe cleaners can be braided to make a handle.

Easter Sunday celebrations can include attendance at worship, an egg hunt for the children, and perhaps a dinner for company. Ham with cherry sauce (pie filling), sweet potatoes, vegetables, and salad, with the basket cake for dessert will make an attractive meal.

ASCENSION DAY FORTY DAYS AFTER EASTER

This holiday is most noted by Roman Catholics, Anglicans, and Eastern Orthodox churches. It is the time for remembering the ascension of Christ into heaven after his resurrection and the appearances to the disciples over a forty-day period. Some churches light a Paschal candle, the symbol of the risen Christ on Easter, and continue to burn it on days of worship until the celebration of this holiday when Acts 1:6-11 is read aloud, and the candle is extinguished.

The ascension was believed to have occurred at Mt. Olivet in Jerusalem. A legend claims that there is a footprint of Jesus in a rock on the spot commemorating this event. A church was built over it during the fourth century but was later destroyed by Muslims. Today there is an octagonal structure surrounding it, and a small number of visitors may enter at a time to view the imprint.

Ascension Day is not mentioned in any written documents until about the fourth century. However, tradition holds that it was celebrated much earlier than that. During the Middle Ages it was a processional day with people carrying torches and banners symbolizing Christ's triumph. Large figures of Christ were made sometimes and raised through a hole in the ceiling while an effigy of the devil descended at the same time.

A more ancient celebration at this time of year honored Roman gods with a flower festival, which led to a custom in England of covering wells with flowers. This celebration may explain the Portuguese custom of gathering bouquets of flowers in order to insure peace, wealth, and good crops for the harvest.

Though Ascension Day is seldom celebrated in the United States, the early Pennsylvania Dutch regarded it as a no-work day; so among the men, it came to be known as fishing day. Superstitions arose against sewing for fear of lightning striking, and sweeping the floor was forbidden lest fleas or ants descend upon the house. Drinks made from herbal teas and consumed on this day were believed to ward off illness for the rest of the year.

The Gospels do not give us a clear account of the ascension. Instead, Matthew describes one brief appearance of Jesus to the disciples (28:16-20) with no mention of the ascension. Mark and John are also silent on the matter. Luke describes several resurrection appearances in chapter 24, then in verse 51 says, "While he blessed

62

them he parted from them and was carried up into heaven." The event seems to have occurred on Easter day. This presents a curious inconsistency, for in the Book of Acts the event is described as happening forty days later. Some scholars suggest that Luke did describe Christ ascending on Easter but continuing to appear for forty days until his final parting in the Book of Acts. Perhaps Luke, as author of both books, is merely recording differing perceptions on this matter.

ASCENSION DAY IN SUNDAY SCHOOL

One tradition associated with this day is decorating churches and homes with FLOWERS. Children might do this by designing a worship tablecloth which has flowers colored with embroidery paint. A cross made from heavy cardboard could be placed on the altar. Real or paper flowers then should be glued onto it. A more permanent cross could be made from two logs and covered with poultry wire. The flowers are poked into the wire all over the cross.

As an alternate activity, children could make an Ascension Day BANNER for the wall, using a footprint (by tracing a child's foot) plus a cross and Paschal candle. A bouquet of fresh flowers or a blooming plant along with a Bible opened to Matthew 6:28-33 (consider the lilies of the field), and the Paschal candle will complete the setting beneath the banner.

Divide the children into two or more groups to STUDY one of the post-resurrection stories of Jesus. These may be found in Matthew 28, Luke 24, and John 20 and 21. Each group will decide on a way to present their story to the class, whether through drama, mural, or story slides.

When the activities are completed, each group will share what they have done. The teacher can read about Ascension Day from Acts 1:6-9. Then the class can worship together.

Worship

Leader: Today is Ascension Day and the end of Jesus' earthly ministry. The Easter (Paschal) candle is lit for the last time today. This is also a day for flowers in the church. Jesus talked about them. We can read it in Matthew 6:28-33.

Sing together: "For the Beauty of the Earth" (Allow children opportunities now to share something important which Jesus taught.)

Share a prayer of love for the church. Extinguish the Paschal candle and pass around the offering plate or basket filled with flowers asking each child to take one in remembrance of what Jesus taught us.

ASCENSION DAY IN FAMILIES

Invite children to prepare for a family remembrance of this day by sharing in putting away any Easter decorations which are still on display around the home. Cleaning, dusting, and decorating the rooms with fresh FLOWERS should follow. Set the dinner table and place one candle in the center to represent the Paschal candle; it should be lit during dinner.

As the meal is being eaten, talk about Ascension Day in the church, and about the wonder of springtime. Share together all the things it is possible to do now that days are warmer. Enjoy HERBAL TEA, a traditional drink for this day.

Before dessert is eaten, read Acts 1:6-11 together, extinguish the Paschal candle, and pray a prayer for Jesus' ministry in the world. Then enjoy a light spring dessert.

Ambrosia Pie

1 pkge. (3 oz.) gelatin—any flavor
1 pkge. (3 ¼ oz.) vanilla pudding (not instant)

2½ c. water
Prepared whipped cream or whipped dairy substitute
1 unbaked coconut pie crust

Combine gelatin, vanilla pudding, and water in a saucepan. Cook and stir over medium heat until mixture boils and becomes clear. Remove from heat and chill until it begins to set. Fold the whipped cream into the pudding and spoon it into the pie shell. Chill for several hours.

Coconut Crust

2½ c. flaked coconut   ⅓ c. margarine

Melt oleo in skillet. Add the coconut and sauté, stirring until it becomes golden in color. Press this into a 9" pie pan, forming a crust. Allow it to stand for at least 30 minutes before filling it.

PENTECOST FIFTY DAYS AFTER EASTER

This name comes from a Greek word meaning fifty and thus is celebrated fifty days after Easter as the birthday of the church. It is a time to remember the experience of the followers of Jesus who had gathered together for a celebration of Pentecost or *Shavuoth* as it is usually called by the Jews.

What happened in Acts 2:1-6 was certainly unexpected: they were "filled with the Holy Spirit." This energized the believers so much that they reportedly baptized about three thousand people (Acts 2:41). Perhaps we can't be certain exactly how they experienced God's gifts. The Book of Acts describes it in colorful, artistic language. One thing is obvious: That day a band of twelve apostles (Matthias having replaced Judas) changed from frightened men into a powerful group of evangelists such as the world had never heard.

Because of the many converts won, it soon became popular to perform baptisms (and later confirmations) on Pentecost. The wearing of white robes later accompanied the ritual of baptism, thereby leading to its second name of White Sunday or Whitsunday. The liturgical color of vestments and altar cloths today, however, is red, commemorating the "tongues of fire" or the presence of the Holy Spirit.

Among Jews, this day (popularly called Feast of Weeks) signals the end of Passover season. Originally a barley harvest, it later was referred to as "law day" or the receiving of the ten commandments, thus making it the birthday of the Jewish faith and their acceptance of a covenant with God. How appropriate it is indeed to celebrate the birthday of Christianity on this same holiday.

Many customs have developed around Pentecost. In Italy, rose petals were rained down on congregations from church roofs, probably symbolic of the Holy Spirit. Three branches were strewn on the floor. French people blew trumpets during mass to remember the violent winds of the Holy Spirit, and let loose dozens of doves (symbols of the Holy Spirit). In England, special offerings, called smoke or hearth money, were given. The amount was determined by how many hearths or chimneys a household had. Favorite foods became cheesecake, baked custard, roast veal, and gooseberry pudding. Cheese dishes are also associated with the Jewish celebration of their "Pentecost."

In worship services today, liturgical dancers wearing bright red and carrying long colorful streamers, accompanied by music, scripture reading, and sounds of wind, can present a moving depiction of Pentecost.

Cheesecake

2   8 oz. packages cream cheese,   4   eggs
    softened   1   6 oz. package chocolate
¾   c. sugar   chips, optional
½   c. sour cream   1¾ c. cookie crumbs
1½ tsp. vanilla   ⅓   c. melted butter or
                                         margarine

Prepare crust of graham cracker crumbs, vanilla wafers, or oreo cookies (1¾ cups of crumbs) and ⅓ cup melted margarine. Place in a pan, pressing it against the edges and bottom until firm.

Beat cream cheese until smooth; add sugar, vanilla, sour cream, and eggs, mixing well. Now you may add a six-ounce package of chocolate chips or 2 tablespoons of unsweetened cocoa and mix until blended. Pour mixture into the crust and bake at 350° until set.

TOPPING:
1   c. sour cream   ¾   c. sugar
1   tsp. vanilla   2   tsp. lemon juice

Blend all ingredients together. Pour over the cake and bake an additional 5 minutes.

PENTECOST IN SUNDAY SCHOOL SETTINGS

One creative way to experience this day is to involve children in a celebration during worship followed by an all-church BIRTHDAY PARTY. On the Saturday before, children and teachers could bake, frost, and decorate cakes. If each participant is asked to bring either cake mix, eggs, or frosting, this will eliminate expenses to the church.

While cakes are baking and cooling, children will have time to make banners, mobiles, and other items needed to celebrate Pentecost.

Suggested BANNER ideas include the cross and flame symbol, a banner with many flames, or one with doves, cross, and flame. Banners should be mounted to a long dowel with a pole attached for carrying them into the sanctuary to be hung. Pinwheels made of bright red paper are easy for younger children to make and carry.

Mobiles may also be made, some with doves, and others with crêpe paper streamers attached to wire poles for mounting on a stand.

Pinwheel

Cut out the square, and in toward the center. Attach points 1, 3, 5, 7 to the center for pinwheel. It may be pinned to the eraser part of a pencil with a straight pin or to a ¼" dowel.

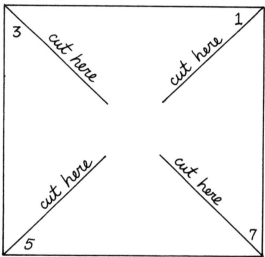

Children might also practice the music for the next day and learn rhythmic DANCE movements to a Pentecost song. Included in the morning would be some rehearsal time for their sharing in a PROCESSION into the sanctuary. This should include choir, children carrying banners, mobiles, the Christian flag, and pinwheels. There might even be a few children blowing bubbles. Children or a group doing a liturgical dance would greatly enhance the celebration, while one child could read the morning scripture verses.

Following worship, a birthday party in the social hall with cakes, balloons, and even clowns would render this a memorable day for all.

An alternate idea would be to have an intergenerational day or evening where people of all ages could study the story of Pentecost, make Holy Spirit collages and MURALS, and sing songs of the season. Holy Spirit WIND CHIMES are a fun idea and may be made by purchasing pieces of cut glass from a glass company. They may be squares, rectangles, or other shapes. These can be painted with acrylic paints, with heavy thread attached to them (the glass company might make tiny holes in each one to make attachment easier). Attach the glass to circular embroidery hoops and hang them where they will chime.

Mobile Chimes

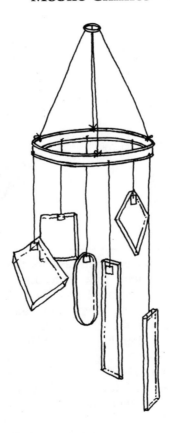

Participants would work in different groups and then come together to share experiences, worship together, and enjoy birthday cake.

PENTECOST IN FAMILY SETTINGS

Invite one or more other church families to your home to celebrate the "birthday of the church." Serve SPICY or colorful FOOD. Use red napkins, placemats, and candles at the table. Children might even decorate the placemats by fingerpainting visions of the Holy Spirit on white paper. A favor cup covered with red crêpe paper and a dove will symbolize the Holy Spirit. The dining room might have crêpe paper streamers across the ceiling as well as on the table.

If it is warm enough, you might have an outdoor party with lots of wind chimes and Chinese lanterns to create a more festive appearance.

With other families, share the special meaning of your faith, read the scripture related to Pentecost, and talk about the birthday of your particular congregation as well.

Share the importance of BIRTHDAYS in families and other times of year when we celebrate birthdays: Independence Day, Labor Day, Christmas, etc. Serve a special birthday cake for dessert.

Easy Pentecost Cake

One prepared round angelfood cake that has a hole in the middle. With a sharp knife cut through the cake horizontally, creating two doughnut shapes. From the topside of the doughnut shape scoop out pieces of cake in small chunks.

Mix fresh or frozen strawberries, whipped topping and the acquired chunks of cake together. Fill in the cake scoops and the center circle of the cake with this mixture. Put the layers back together and frost with more whipped topping. Add candles for a Pentecost cake.

Mother's Day

A woman named Anna Jarvis from Philadelphia is credited with the modern-day celebration of Mother's Day. In 1907 she planned a special worship service to honor all moms, and parishioners wore white carnations to mark the day.

The following year other churches adopted the idea; and, before long, the day was celebrated in every state as well as in Canada, Mexico, China, plus African, South American, and European nations.

In 1913 the House of Representatives voted the second Sunday in May officially as Mother's Day and called upon all officials to display the flag and to wear white carnations in honor of moms everywhere.

Today red carnations are often worn by persons whose mothers are living, and the white carnation has been chosen to represent those moms now deceased.

Gift giving, card purchasing, and taking Mom out to lunch or having large family gatherings (often with Mom doing the cooking) have become part of the celebration.

Motherhood festivals do have an ancient origin, however, dating back to the Greeks' worship of Cybile, the mother of gods who was honored in special religious rites once a year in March. These rituals bore no resemblance to our modern-day celebrations.

Mother's Day is a time when special concern can be shown in congregations for the needs of mothers everywhere. For example, many of the "new poor" we see today are from single-parent families, mothers with their children. Today we no longer think of the homeless as skid row alcoholics. High rents and low paying jobs or no jobs have forced whole families onto the streets and into temporary tent cities across the nation.

Your congregation might receive a special offering on this day to help with this problem. Organizations such as WIC (Women, Infants, Children) and others (perhaps a women's shelter in your community) need funds to assist displaced families. A novel idea used in our congregation was to collect from each person as many pennies as their mother was old. While this may not seem complimentary, it did generate an offering in a creative manner.

The gift of red carnations, given in the worship service to all mothers, is another idea. Moms might serve as ushers and liturgists in the service. One of the most moving sermons I've ever heard was shared by three mothers (a brand new mother, a mother with elementary-age children, and a mother of a teenager). Each shared the joys, pains, and special moments of motherhood, lending extra meaning to the congregation's worship.

Another idea is to invite members of the congregation, children included, to send in a statement (a couple of sentences are sufficient) on what their mom means to them. These could be printed up as extra pages and inserted into the Sunday bulletin.

In some churches mother-daughter banquets are often held during May. In honor of mothers, an all-male choir (recruited from the congregation) sings the morning anthem, giving mothers who are regularly in the choir the morning off.

Often Mother's Day brings extra visitors to your worship service, as grown children return home and grandparents come to visit. These guests need to be recognized by the congregation. Perhaps a new tradition could be started by giving a pink carnation to the visiting mothers.

Festival of the Christian Home

United Methodists, as well as other denominations, in an effort to assist the celebration of Mother's Day, declared the first week of May to be the celebration of the Festival of the Christian Home. The title was revised later to be called National Family Week. It is a time when the church needs to make a conscious effort to focus on the needs and relationships of families, including itself as a church family.

Your church might sponsor a series of potluck suppers for your "church family," with time for fellowship and learning. Explore together better ways to relate to the different styles of family life found today: single-parent families, unmarried adults living together, and whatever other family styles you have in your church and community.

Educational opportunities focusing on parenting skills and marriage relationships might be a part of your learning time. Local schools, pastors, and Christian educators can often provide or help find leadership and speakers.

An intergenerational church school with all ages meeting together to study, learn, and experience fellowship is also an idea for the month of May. Sunday school lesson ideas are available through Christian bookstores, or you may develop your own session plans. Classes which begin with elementary-age children and go through adults usually work better than those including younger children. A learning center teaching style is one way to provide a variety of choices for your participants.

You might plan a worship celebration which focuses on values and family life and involves a number of families in the planning and participation.

Mother's Day and the Festival of the Christian Home in Church Settings

It is important to know the family status of children in your church before embarking on special experiences for Mother's Day, since not all children live with their mothers. Be sensitive to children's situations.

In the short time of a Sunday morning class, it may be difficult to make a Mother's Day GIFT; so you may decide to have a Saturday work party. Since Father's Day is in June during school vacation, you might also make Dad's gift at this time. For children without one or more parents, make something for someone whom they love as much as a parent.

Begin your Saturday class with STORIES of special mothers and families in the Bible:

Sara and Abraham, parents of Isaac, Genesis 2:1-6
Elizabeth and Zechariah, parents of John the Baptist, Luke 1:5-80
Mary and Joseph, parents of Jesus, Luke 2:1-19

Perhaps your church or denomination has an important founding family. An important family to United Methodists is that of Susannah and Samuel Wesley, parents of nineteen children. Susannah's dedication to family discipline and methodical ways inspired son John's strict manners and religious fervor, while all the sons were to follow religious lives similar to their parents. John inspired a new religious movement; and Charles, a preacher also, wrote over 6,000 hymns.

After sharing these stories, children can discuss the importance of their parents in their lives. The class then might write litany prayers for parents, using a refrain such as, "We thank you, God, for our families."

Since this is also the time the church celebrates the Festival of the Christian Home, the class might DISCUSS TELEVISION FAMILIES and share ways in which they are like or unlike their own. A discussion of TV versus the real world can reveal expectations and false attitudes which children often develop from the media.

Gift making will come next. You undoubtedly have ideas of your own, but here are a few you might consider:

For POTPOURRI, flower and leaf petals must be dried ahead of time. Use bright-colored flowers, especially fragrant ones; roses are the easiest to dry and give the variety of color needed, but other spring flowers can also be used.

Flowers picked early in the day are more fragrant if picked after the morning dew has evaporated.

To air-dry petals, place petals which have been broken apart onto a screen so ventilation from both sides is possible. Allow three to four weeks drying time by turning them every few days. When dry, store in a glass jar in a darkened area to preserve the colors.

To oven dry, spread petals on a cookie sheet or in a glass cake pan and turn the oven to 150°, allowing them to dry overnight, longer if you live in a damp climate.

To dry in a microwave, make a mixture of 2 cups borax to 1 cup sand. Lay petals on this mixture, add a glass of water to the oven, and microwave for 1 minute (or longer if needed).

Recipe for potpourri:

1	quart dried petals (flowers and leaves)	½	oz. ground cinnamon
2	oz. orris root (purchase in a natural foods store)	4	oz. salt
2	oz. ground coriander	½	oz. flower oil (available in craft stores)

The children may measure and mix the potpourri ingredients.

To make a sachet: Small embroidery hoops, net in pretty colors or other thin fabric, lace, ribbon, and small silk flowers are needed.

Insert one circle of net or fabric 1″ wider than the hoop between the two hoops as you would do with embroidery material. Turn to the underside of the hoop and fill the cavity with the potpourri mixture. Glue fabric or more net to fit the hoop to the back side of the frame with glue from a glue gun or other craft glue. Add a circle of lace approximately ¾″ to 1″ wide around the back of the hoop. Ribbon and flowers may be added to the front side along with a decal if desired. At the top a loop of ribbon glued to the back will serve as a hanger.

Paper CARNATIONS are simple to make; each flower requires only one piece of facial tissue. To make, open the tissue and cut it in half the long way. Put the two halves together and accordion fold them. When folded, tie the end of a pipe cleaner across the middle of the folded tissue for a stem. Then fluff out the folded parts of the tissue until it hides the center and takes on a flower appearance.

Greeting CARDS may be made to resemble a bouquet of flowers. Under each flower can be written a special chore which the child promises to do, such as mow the lawn, dust, wash dishes, etc. When Mom receives the card, she may cut one flower off the card each day during the week, and the child will be responsible for that chore.

Your class might also adopt an older, perhaps widowed, mother whose children are grown and do not live nearby and prepare a special treat for her. Cookies, greeting cards, or even a lunch might be prepared and taken to her as part of your work party.

An ambitious class might ADOPT A FAMILY in need and find an appropriate way to help with canned foods, special offering, or other types of service.

On Sunday morning invite a mother and new baby to visit and share with children her experiences of being a mother.

Some churches choose this time of year to present a children's choir musical, which is appropriate when families often have grandparents visiting.

A cake decorating contest where children of all ages decorate a CAKE for Mom or the church family is a fun activity. Cakes may be homemade or purchased in a store, but all decorating must be done by the children. Display the cakes prior to the musical and judge them. Be certain that each child receives recognition for some category (prettiest, funniest, most colorful, etc). Cakes may be eaten by guests at the conclusion of the children's program.

Of course, you will want to include stepmoms in all of the teaching and gift-making ideas. See also the ideas for dads and stepdads included in the chapter on Father's Day.

MOTHER'S DAY AND FESTIVAL OF THE CHRISTIAN HOME IN FAMILY SETTINGS

Whether you are a family that is large or small, has two parents or one, or is an extended family, you can celebrate this day as a time for loving each other and being together.

A way to honor Mom in the morning is for the family to keep her from the kitchen while the rest of the members prepare a special BREAKFAST for her. Hotcakes, sausage, orange juice, and coffee are easy to prepare and Mom will appreciate the luxurious service. A carnation on the breakfast tray or table with a crown for Mom would add to the special treat.

A CROWN can be made with a piece of tagboard approximately 23" long (allow 1" for stapling the two edges together). It needs to be cut with a peak in the front and smaller peaks on the sides. It may be sprayed with gold paint and small jewels glued onto it. Bits of old jewelry will work well for this. Dad or some other adult might plan ahead with the children for a notebook of pictures (photos and drawings, and words of praise) to present to Mom as her *Notebook of Memories.*

A family PICNIC (weather permitting) might alleviate the need for a large family dinner and provide a setting for a celebration of family togetherness. Rainy day picnics are fun also and can be held in the family room, covered porch, or basement of a house.

Open face SANDWICHES are a Scandinavian tradition and can be taken to a picnic when stored in plastic containers. They are always pretty and attractive and include less bread and more filling.

Bread is spread with butter or mayonnaise and then the prepared topping. Tuna or egg salad, sliced meat, or cheese make good sandwiches. These may be topped with a garnish of sliced radish, cucumber, tomato, carrot curl, or piece of shrimp or sardines. The garnish should look attractive and lend color to the sandwich. These may be stored in plastic containers, with a piece of waxed paper separating each sandwich.

Fruit, beverages, and a dessert of cookies or cake can be taken along.

Orange Cake

Use a package of white or yellow cake mix and substitute orange juice for water in the recipe. Add 3 to 4 tbl. of grated orange rind. Follow the rest of the recipe according to directions on the package. Frost the cake with white icing and add orange slices for color.

The family day together might conclude a short worship time of scripture reading on appreciation (1 Corinthians 13:4-7) and a prayer of thankfulness for the love which we have for each other.

FATHER'S DAY

THIRD SUNDAY IN JUNE

The beginnings of this holiday lack the clarity associated with Mother's Day, since several people in different parts of the country, unknown to each other, believed that they had originated the idea. However a Mrs. John Dodd of Spokane, Washington seems to have been the first to do so in June 1909. She wanted a day to celebrate and thank her own dear father who raised his children alone after her mother died. As on Mother's Day, flowers were worn—a red rose in honor of a living father and a white rose to honor a deceased father.

The next year a celebration of fathers was discussed in Chicago by Jane Addams with no results; but in 1913, people in Vancouver, Washington celebrated the day through the efforts of a Methodist pastor. Though the first Father's Day was celebrated in June, an October date was chosen in 1920 in Chicago.

President Coolidge once wrote a letter in support of the day as a time when fathers ought to be reminded of their full obligations to their families. However, the first time a resolution to establish a national Father's Day was presented to Congress, it failed the necessary votes for passage. Today it is as popular as Mother's Day. Gift and card giving are an expected custom.

CELEBRATING FATHER'S DAY IN CHURCH SETTINGS

There are many ways to celebrate this holiday in worship settings: an all-female choir, sermons about fatherhood, and statements (by fathers and/or children). Children in our church presented helium-filled balloons saying, "A father is to love," to each adult male after the worship service on that day.

In the Sunday school classroom, teachers should be sensitive to the fact that some children do not live with their natural fathers and may have conflicting feelings about the day. These can best be addressed by talking honestly with each child and getting his or her feelings about it.

There are some good STORIES in the Bible about fathers that you might wish to share in class:

Abraham who was afraid he loved his son more than God (Genesis: chapters 21-22)

76

Isaac who had twin sons Jacob and Esau (Genesis 25-27)

Jacob the father of twelve sons, whose favorite, Joseph, was sent to slavery in Egypt through the jealousy of his brothers (Genesis 29-30, 37-47)

Jesus whose parable of the prodigal son (also titled, "The Forgiving Father") leads us to believe he must have experienced a special loving relationship with his earthly father, Joseph. You might use the parable in class to emphasize God's all-powerful love for us, being careful to add that God is like the most loving person you know, for the benefit of those children who cannot relate the concept of a loving father to God.

Father's Day CARDS are fun and easy to make. Some suggested designs are a paper necktie with yarn attached to the top, painted with sponge paint or colored tissue paper. If it opens up, a message can be on the inside. A card in the shape of a shirt, also painted, can have shirt buttons glued onto it, and makes a practical gift.

For a child who wishes to send a Father's Day greeting to a dad who doesn't live with him or her, trace on butcher paper the outstretched arms, shoulders, and hands of the child. The child may then cut it out and put a message on the paper such as, "I love you this much," or, "This is my hug for you." Children also can make ribbons or construction paper badges which say "Father of the Year" for Dad to wear on this day.

Children might also write their letters of love and appreciation to their fathers and include promises of a job they will do to help Dad at home this week.

Older boys and girls might like to interview fathers in the church by asking them to finish a sentence such as, "The most special thing about my being a father is . . . " These can be gathered and put into a booklet or written up and placed in the church newsletter.

FATHER'S DAY IN FAMILY SETTINGS

Families can make this an important day for Dad by preparing his favorite meal. Children can share in the cooking.

Make a special CROWN of cardboard for Dad to wear as "King" for a day. This he might wear during dinner.

Most fathers enjoy sweets. One large COOKIE made by children and decorated is a fun way to present dessert. Use your favorite drop cookie recipe or make a chocolate chip cookie following the recipe on the package of chocolate chips. Then oil the bottom and sides of a 9" cake pan and spread enough batter to cover the bottom of the pan, approximately ½" thick. Allow it to bake at 375° about 15 minutes or until lightly brown. Remove the pan from the oven and let it sit for a minute or two, then remove your cookie from the pan. Slip it onto a wire rack and let cool. Then decorate with frosting around the edges, using a decorator kit, and write, "LOVE YOU, DAD," on the cookie.

Mom and the children can also make up a CASSETTE tape message ahead of time, telling dad what is special about him and recalling important family events. This can then be shared on Father's Day.

For families in which there is no father present, but Dad is still much a part of the child's life, it is important to help children deal with any unkind feelings other family members may have and allow the child freedom to express feelings of love and appreciation to Dad. In this case, a phone call or a day to visit Dad may be important parts of the celebration.

Stepdads often present feelings of conflict and even guilt to a child who may need to be allowed to do what he or she feels best about in choosing one or both men to be special dads. In any case, the child should be freed from feelings of guilt. Words such as "It's okay to have two dads today," or "I understand you want to be with your first dad today, and that's okay. I can be your other dad tomorrow," will help with this.

It might be in your family that dad would prefer to be taken out on a "surprise" TRIP, perhaps to a sporting event. Why not blindfold dad, direct him to the car, and take him to his surprise outing for the day? However you celebrate, it's important for Dad to feel appreciated and loved on this special day.

INDEPENDENCE DAY JULY 4

It was on July 2, 1776 that the Continental Congress of the thirteen colonies adopted a resolution proposed by Richard Henry Lee "that these united colonies are, and of a right ought to be, free and independent." Prior to this day five members of a committee had worked on a formal draft (largely written by Thomas Jefferson) of what would become known as the Declaration of Independence. It would be signed by representatives from all the colonies by August 2, 1776.

Opposition to English rule began in 1761 when the colony of Massachusetts led by James Otis spoke against the British Writs of Assistance. Various other attempts by England to control the colonies (as part of English belief they existed to enhance the motherland) were met with resistance. The make-up of the colonies by a breed of independent thinkers, often people who could not get along in their homeland or who sought freedom from religious persecution, was not one to tolerate excessive taxation. Opposition continued through Great Britain's many attempts at control and resulted in the Boston massacre: British soldiers fired upon a mob of stone-throwing citizens, causing several deaths. On December 16, 1773, a group of citizens, thinly disguised as Indians and declaring they would not pay one penny for taxation, dumped an entire shipment of tea into the Boston Harbor. This bold act led to the establishment of the Intolerable Acts, and the battles of Lexington and Concord. Soon a full-fledged war was led by George Washington, then a wealthy Virginia farmer.

The Declaration of Independence originally contained a segment denouncing slavery, which was deleted unfortunately from the final document. As it stands today, there are three principal parts: a preamble with a statement of the natural rights of all people, a middle portion with twenty-eight grievances against King George III, and a last section containing Lee's declaration. It has 56 signers, the largest signature being that of John Hancock. The signing was costly for some who knew that they could never return to England. A few lost their fortunes, and at least one man lost his life because he needed surgery which was obtainable only in England. They signed this document amidst a war in which a third of the population were apathetic, a little less than a third were loyalists, and slightly more than a third were in favor of independence.

It wasn't until 1783 that independence was won and a formal treaty signed in Paris by representatives of both Great Britain and the colonies.

Recognition of Independence Day began before the final separation from England but didn't become widespread until much later. In 1777 it was celebrated in Philadelphia by bell ringing, bonfires, and fireworks. Ships in nearby harbors fired a thirteen-gun salute, and lighted candles were placed in windows. The first official recognition of Independence Day was declared by Massachusetts in 1781.

On the fiftieth anniversary of the day, special ceremonies were held; and all former presidents and signers were invited to participate. However, John Adams and Thomas Jefferson, who had earlier declined, both died on this day. It would be five years later to the day James Monroe would also die.

Throughout our history, this day has been marked by parades, military salutes, fireworks, and special government presentations. Speeches, flag waving, and re-enactments of the nation's history have also been part of the important celebration.

Our early beginning as a nation was shaky, and it took forming a Constitution with a strong central government to pull it together. James Madison is often called the father of this document. While fifty-five men worked on it, only forty-two remained to sign it, having decided it would become law when two-thirds of the states would agree to it. The Constitution, with the Bill of Rights, initiated the most amazing change in government the world had ever known, although those who worked on it were never really satisfied with its contents.

One of the most important rights was the establishment of freedom of religion and separation of church and state. This removed from protection the state (Congregational) churches in all of New England except Rhode Island and the Anglican Church as official church in several other states. More than any other document in history, this bill opened the way for greater religious freedom and toleration. It is indeed a holiday of importance to churches all across the land, and one in which many forms of celebration may occur. Methodism, as much as any religious group, has its development and growth rooted in the history of this land.

Our newly founded nation was by no means homogeneous. Even at the beginning, we had greater ethnic, religious, and national diversity than any other country in the world, and we have continued to diversify ever since. We can be immensely proud that we are a people of differences and indeed have incorporated the traditions, ideas, and talents of many into what is called the U.S.A. today.

INDEPENDENCE DAY IN WORSHIP AND SUNDAY SCHOOL SETTINGS

An intergenerational Sunday school and worship celebrating American religious traditions will help children and adults understand the religious foundations of this nation. Worship could be a Puritan New England service, Methodist Camp Meeting, or silent Quaker service.

Puritan Worship Service

Pastors, ushers (to be called tithingmen), greeters, and all other participants in worship should dress in clothing of the 1700s. One man will be needed as the town crier. By ringing his bell, he will call the congregation to worship. "Hear ye, hear ye, worship will begin in five minutes," might be a typical cry. Printed bulletins will help the congregation understand the style and mood of the service. One is included with comments and suggestions:

Order of Publick Worship 1776
Colony of Massachusetts

Organ Prelude—Choose music which is somber and foreboding.

Opening Prayer—All standing with arms raised overhead in adoration and receptiveness to God.

Opening Hymn—"All Hail the Power of Jesus' Name" (or other hymn of ancient origin). Churches did not have hymn books, so the choir director will sing each line first and allow the congregation to respond.

Reading from the Bible—The public reading of scripture without comment was called dumb reading. Therefore please add comments as scripture is read.

Time of Censure and Announcement—Issue reprimands to imaginary people for wrongdoings such as "Mother Anabelle was required to sit in the stocks for four hours on Monday for

speaking unkindly to a neighbor. She is truly repentant." This
was also a time to share civic and social concerns since everyone
in town was a church member and expected to attend church
services. References could be made here to the oppression of
England and refusal to pay taxes.
Prayer of Confession—Puritans often stood for one hour for this
prayer time.
Sermon—Obtain an old sermon of Jonathan Edwards from the
library or write one with lots of the solemn reprimands which
were common to sermons of that day. Sermons would often last
3-4 hours, and persons would spontaneously participate with
"Amens" and other comments.
Offertory—Tithingpersons will receive the offering.
Closing hymn—Congregation standing (Teach this hymn as you
did the first one.)
Benediction and Postlude

During the service, several tithingmen should wander through the
congregation and with long poles, tickle the foreheads of anyone who
dares to doze. Background information of interest to the congregation
(for the back page of the bulletin):
   In colonial days, Puritan places of worship were called meeting
houses since there is no reference in scripture to "churches." They
were rarely painted and were extremely austere inside—extravagance
being avoided. Windows were made of clear glass, and early pews of
long wooden planks without backs, often rested on milk cans. Later
the concept of family pews developed, backs were included, and pews
were enclosed with little doors. These were paid for and maintained
by their "owners."
   At first, a call to worship was announced by blowing on a conch
shell. Later, bells were rung; and drums sounded. In Plymouth
Colony, the flag was displayed. During some periods of history, men
and women sat on opposite sides of the meeting house; and seats
were assigned on the basis of one's status in the community. The most
important people received locations nearest the heater in winter and
the windows in summer. Worship was an all-day experience with
long prayers, even longer sermons, and breaks for lunch, as well as

time to water the horses both morning and afternoon. People tended to doze, so a tithingman with a long pole, which had a knob on one end and a feather on the other, could remind them to stay awake and focus on the sermon. Men attended with their weapons, left first, and after determining it was safe, allowed women and children to follow.

INTERGENERATIONAL CHURCH SCHOOL

This should be held in a large room or social hall which is divided into interest and activity areas for everyone.
Suggestions follow:

1. *Stocks*—Built by a member of the congregation. Allow people to be photographed here.
2. *Candle Dipping Center*—An opportunity to observe and make a candle. (Save and melt down old wedding candles to use here.)
3. *Antique Area*—Items of colonial America on loan by members or from a local antique shop.
4. *Wool Carding*—Spinning and dyeing demonstration.
5. *Cooking*—Over an open fire out of doors or in a fireplace.

Study centers could include the following:

1. Speaker on the blue laws (information available at the library).
2. Pilgrim Puritan history lesson—Sharing interesting facts. Include here the making of bonnets and collars.
3. Film or filmstrip on early U.S. history from public or judicatory film library.
4. Shaker Study Group—This group could learn the song "Tis the Gift to Be Simple" and teach it to the congregation.
5. Early Quaker Beginnings—Quaker worship or perhaps a skit could be developed here.

Many other religious groups and traditions from other colonies might become part of this study. A study of "Religion in America" could be continued for several weeks. The last 20 minutes of class time would be a sharing by all groups and closing hymn. "My Country, 'Tis of Thee" would be an excellent choice.

An old-fashioned American Camp Meeting is a way to celebrate Methodist beginnings. This should include a lot of hymn singing using the Wesley songs, or "There's a Meetin' Here Tonight," "Amazing Grace," and others.

Share the Methodist rules for singing written by John Wesley (found in the *Book of Hymns*, 1964, p. viii), a sermon with a Peter Cartwright style, followed by an altar call, prayers, and more music to conclude the service. Hand clapping, hallelujahs, and amens should be part of the enthusiastic service.

An American celebration of Independence Day with softball game, horseshoes, log sawing contest, watermelon eating contest, tug of war, relay races, gunny sack race, seed spitting contest, and wheelbarrow race are suggestions. Members of the congregation can bring foods to share, and homemade ice cream can be the dessert. A country fair is another idea with exhibits of handiwork, crocheted items, quilts, canned foods, wood projects, and rock collections. These can be judged—all adding to the celebration.

Homemade Ice Cream

Scald 3 qt. of light cream and 3 c. of whole milk together.
Add: 4 well-beaten eggs,
     3 c. sugar
Cook all ingredients until smooth. Add flavoring (2 tbl. vanilla and fruits as desired). Beat, blend, and freeze in an electric ice cream freezer.

INDEPENDENCE DAY IN FAMILIES

Celebrate this day with a backyard picnic, beach party, or neighborhood BLOCK PARTY. In some places it is possible, with permission from the police department, to close off an entire street and hold the party on front lawns and in the street. Neighbors and other guests will enjoy participating in such an event. Reserving space in a neighborhood park or beach is an alternative to this.

All guests should wear red, white, and blue CLOTHING or else be dressed in a costume of their favorite hero or heroine. Assign each person the name of one President and ask them to share something about him.

Many GAMES can be played by all ages—croquet, badminton, relay races, three-legged races, hopscotch, marbles, jacks, water-balloon toss, and others. Charades could be played using famous quotations such as, "Give me liberty or give me death" (Patrick Henry). "Give me your tired, your poor, your huddled masses yearning to breathe free" (Emma Lazarus). "Ask not what your country can do for you but rather what you can do for your country" (John F. Kennedy).

Music of America is another idea. SINGING a variety of songs together and participating in square dances and the Virginia Reel would be fun.

A POTLUCK meal could be provided by assigning every family a different state and requesting that they provide typical foods from there. Suggestions might include fried chicken (Kentucky); baked beans (Massachusetts); Cajun food (Louisiana); barbecued beef (Texas); etc. An alternate idea would be to assign each family foods of different ethnic groups. The variety of foods would be wonderful indeed.

Patriotic Jello

1 small pkg. red jello	1 envelope unflavored jello
2 c. liquid (hot)	3 tbl. sugar
fruit (raspberries or strawberries)	2 c. hot liquid
Prepare and put in a mold, chill;	blueberries (some juice may go
1 small container sour cream	into the liquid)
Spread sour cream over the jello	1 tbl. lemon juice
when it is set.	Blend ingredients and add to rest of
	the jello, chill.

Baked Alaska

9"   round cake, any flavor   ½   tsp. cream of tartar
2   qt. ice cream   1   c. sugar
6   large egg whites

Pack ice cream in round bowl 8" in diameter. Chill until very hard. Beat egg whites and cream of tartar, gradually adding sugar. Beat until meringue is very stiff and glossy. Heat oven to 500°. Place cooled cake on baking sheet. Loosen ice cream from bowl, place it on top of the cake. Spread meringue around everything, covering ice cream and cake completely. Bake 3 to 5 minutes until meringue is lightly browned. Serve immediately.

LABOR DAY

Holidays to celebrate working men and women are not a recent idea. In ancient Greece, artisans and slaves held parades and carried torches once a year as did guilds in various European countries on their patron saints' days. Today, many socialist and communist countries recognize May 1 as the day on which to honor workers.

The idea for Labor Day in the United States was a long time in coming and was preceded by many attempts on the part of workers to organize for a fair wage and shorter working hours. The first recorded strike occurred in Philadelphia in 1786 when printers quit their jobs to protest a cut in wages below $6 per week. Then shoemakers of that city founded a workers' organization which dissolved within a year. By 1820 numerous unions had organized but were largely local in nature.

Prior to the Civil War, conditions for workers were especially poor, because of free slave labor and the employment of women and children. After the war, workers began to organize in earnest. By 1872, there were several hundred thousand workers in thirty-two unions. Some 23,000 strikes were reported between 1881 and 1900.

The National Labor Union (1866) lasted only six years but attempted to nationalize organizers and to advocate an eight-hour work day. It was followed by the Knights of Labor which suffered its death blow with the Hay Market Square labor dispute during which someone threw a dynamite bomb, killing a dozen people. This resulted in court trials and several hangings.

Samuel Gompers of Chicago is credited for his leadership of the AFL (American Federation of Labor), and many gains were made under him.

The idea for an official day to honor Labor began with a proposal by Peter J. McGuire in 1882. It was a sign of the times that two years later Congress officially designated the first Monday in September as a legal holiday. It was signed into law by President Grover Cleveland. This date was selected primarily because there were no other holidays on the calendar, and it is a pleasant time of the year.

For many years Labor Day meant huge parades and opportunities for unions to demonstrate their strength. Many workers would march, carrying large signs stating "All men are created equal" and "Vote for the Labor ticket."

Today in much of the United States, Labor Day marks the end of summer, closing down of tourist attractions, and the last day before the return to busy fall activities. It is a time for picnics, short trips, chili cook-offs, parades, and closing down the summer house. Churches sometimes recognize the day by inviting workers to attend worship in workday clothes, and they hold services in which workers are recognized for their work contribution to society.

LABOR DAY IN SUNDAY SCHOOL

Plan to spend some time explaining the historical reason for Labor Day and why it is observed. Then, after consulting concordances, ask children to look up several verses which use the word *labor* to see what the Bible has to say about the subject. Discuss each verse. In the children's own words, make a list on a chalkboard or newsprint of what God is telling us through scripture.

Suggestions for verses.
1. "Six days shall you labor and do all your work, but the seventh day is a Sabbath" (Exodus 20:9).
2. "Unless the Lord builds the house, those who build it labor in vain" (Psalm 127:1).
3. "Come to me all who labor and are heavy laden and I will give you rest" (Matthew 11:28).
4. "He who plants and he who waters are equal, and each shall receive his wages according to his labor. For we are fellow workers for God" (1 Corinthians 3:8-9).
5. "Their hearts were bowed with hard labor, they fell down with none to help. Then they cried to the Lord . . . and God delivered them" (Psalm 107: 12-13).

After discussing the meaning of the verses, children can rewrite them in their own words and make POSTER paintings of them. They should be on stiff paper in large letters. Dowels or flat yardsticks can be attached to the back of each poster with the Bible verse written on the back. Since parades were a part of Labor Day from its inception, these will make good signs to carry.

Plan your PARADE route (around the church property or nearby neighborhood). Consider whether or not to invite other classes to join you. Drums, other instruments, and flags, along with the posters, should give each child something to carry. They might also like to explain to other boys and girls what they have learned about Labor Day.

Before the close of class, talk about what it means to share one's labor for God. Allow children to consider how they do this now and ways in which they might do this when they are grown. A special guest (parent, perhaps) might visit for a few minutes to share how he/she is serving God as a lay person.

End the class time with a special prayer of thanks for all persons who labor to serve God.

LABOR DAY IN FAMILIES

Teaching children the meaning and significance of one's work is an important task for every family, so pause today to talk about your household's OCCUPATIONS or professions. Relate these to ways in which we serve God through our paid jobs as well as in our relationships. Discuss the work we do at the church.

Hold a FAMILY COUNCIL meeting to decide how each family member can contribute to the happiness of everyone. Allow children some voice in choosing which jobs they will do. Decide whether the jobs will be rotated every week.

Read verses from the Bible together and share what they mean. First Corinthians 15:58 and 3:8-9, as well as Matthew 11:28, are suggestions.

If a Labor Day parade is being held nearby, plan to attend and enjoy it together. Some communities in California hold chili cook-offs on this holiday. Here is a less spicy recipe which children often prefer. Allow them to cook today.

American Chili

1	lb. ground beef or turkey	1	tsp. salt
1	medium onion	1	tsp. chili powder (more for
1	bottle ketchup		spicier flavor)
1	(30 oz.) can red beans	¼	tsp. pepper
			sprinkling of garlic salt

Brown onion and meat together. Pour off any fat which might accumulate. Add drained red beans, ketchup, and spices. Simmer for 10 to 15 minutes until the mixture is hot.

WORLD
COMMUNION SUNDAY First Sunday in October

Originally called the Fellowship of Suffering and Service, World Communion Sunday began as a Presbyterian movement in 1936. Its purpose was to express the world-wide fellowship of the church and to strengthen congregational obedience to Christ during the depression years. In 1940 the executive secretary of the National Council of Churches, Dr. Jesse Bader, made this a day of ecumenical importance. Methodist churches in the early 1940s adopted World Communion Sunday as a time for communion and collected special offerings to assist people in war-torn lands. Chaplains and military personnel also received a portion of the offering to assist in establishing Sunday schools and worship facilities.

When the World Council of Churches was formed in 1948, steps were taken to make this day more than a U.S. observance. This did not become a reality until 1967. It became a day to remember our world-wide unity in Christ but inter-communion (sharing between denominations) has never been its intention. It is estimated that the Holy Communion table is 25,000 miles long, with millions of Christians around the globe participating. The day is celebrated by Protestants in many lands, with each denomination preparing its own special materials, prayers, and rituals. It is not generally celebrated by Roman Catholics who celebrate communion every Sunday anyway, or among Orthodox Christians. The day begins on the other side of the International Dateline with the Tongan Islands, Fiji, Australia, and New Zealand, and so on around the globe.

Though Christian unity is not the purpose of the day, it is an ideal time to pray for the unity of all God's people and pray that we will work cooperatively with each other in areas of mission and service around the globe. Some churches have celebrated this day by incorporating different languages in the prayers and ritual of the worship service or by wearing costumes of different countries. "In Christ There Is No East or West" is a popular hymn for congregations to sing. Today, United Methodists, alone, celebrate this day as a time to receive special offerings to assist deserving students around the world.

WORLD COMMUNION SUNDAY
IN SUNDAY SCHOOL SETTINGS

On the day before this holy day, invite children to the church to prepare the communion bread for the congregation's worship. They will find this quite enjoyable if each one can, in addition, make a small loaf of BREAD to take home. It will take time for the dough to rise, giving opportunity for additional learning. Children might begin this session by reading together the communion ritual to be used and discussing its meaning. Music for the service could also be sung. Perhaps the children might even learn a Bible verse in another language to share with the congregation.

In addition, teachers might talk about the special offering if your denomination collects one (United Methodists do); and the children might make large POSTERS advertising this day and the offering. PICTURES of the world's children in native dress is one effective idea. Children will need to help place the completed posters around the church grounds.

They can also share by preparing the communion items, by washing cups, and by cleaning chalices. Should there be time, letters can be written to a church of another denomination in the neighborhood. Focus on the joy of celebrating with others our unity in Christ on this special day. Two or three children would be responsible for delivering the mail personally.

Children dressed in COSTUMES of the world could participate in the worship service as liturgists, ushers, greeters, and acolytes. Some rehearsing time will be needed if this is going to become a part of the day's events.

Plan to say the Lord's PRAYER in at least one other language as a part of worship. It is included here in Spanish.

The Lord's Prayer

PADRE Pah-dray	NUESTRO new-es-troe	QUE kay	ESTAS es-tas	EN in	LOS los	CIELOS see-eh-los
SANTIFICADO san-tee-fee-caw-doe		SEA say-ah	TU too	NOMBRE. nom-bray	VENGA ven-gah	TU too
REINO. ray-noe	HAGASE ah-gah-say	TU too	VOLUNTAD vol-oon-tahd	COMO co-mo	EN in	EL el
CIELO, see-eh-loe	ASI ah-see	TAMBIEN tombee-ayn	EN in	LA la	TIERRA. tee-eh-rah	EL el

PAN	NUESTRO	DE	CADA	DIA,	DANOSLO	HOY	
pahn	new-es-troe	day	cah-dah	dee-ah	dahn-os-lo	oi	
Y	PERDONA	NUESTRAS	DEUDAS	COMO	TAMBIEN		
ee	pear-don-ah	new-es-tras	day-oo-dahs	como	tom-bee-ayn		
PERDONAMOS	A	NUESTROS	DEUDORES.	Y	NO		
pear-don-ah-mos	ah	new-es-tros	day-oo-dor-ehs	ee	no		
NOS	METAS	EN	TENTACION	MAS	LIBRANOS	DEL	
nos	may-tas	in	ten-tah-see-on	mahs	lee-brah-nos	del	
MAL,	PORQUE	TUYO	ES	EL	REINO,	Y	EL
mahl	pour-kay	too-yo	ess	el	ray-noe	ee	el
PODER,	Y	LA	GLORIA	POR	TODOS	LOS	
po-dare	ee	la	glow-ree-ah	pour	toe-dos	los	
SIGLOS.	AMEN.						
see-glos	amen						

Communion Bread

2 pkg. yeast	2 tbsp. sugar
2 tbsp. margarine or butter	2 c. water
2 tsp. salt	7 to 8 c. flour

Dissolve the yeast in ½ cup warm water. Add 2 tsp. sugar and let it stand for 10 minutes.

Warm 2 cups water, 2 tbsp. margarine, 2 tbsp. sugar, and 2 tsp. salt to a temperature of 130°. Cool it to 110°. Mix it together with the yeast and add 2 cups of flour. Mix and add 2 more cups of flour. Drop it onto a breadboard and knead for ten minutes, gradually adding flour and working in up to 7½ cups. If it is sticky, add the additional ½ cup. Allow dough to rise in a warm place for approximately 45 minutes; then punch it down and form it into two round loaves. Place it in a flat baking pan and let it rise an additional 30 minutes. Cut a cross in the center of each loaf. Brush the top with butter or 2 tbsp. of milk mixed with 1 egg. Bake at 425° about 20 minutes.

WORLD COMMUNION SUNDAY WITH FAMILIES

Talk with children about the different denominations of Christians in your community. Share something about each one: ways we are alike, ways we are different, and how we all hold a common faith in Jesus Christ. Talk with one or more neighbors of other denominations about the significance of this day. You might be surprised to discover that not all Christian groups join in this celebration. You might ask them why. Invite a neighbor or relative from another church to your congregation for this Sunday, or make plans to attend their church, provided they have open communion.

Ask your pastor for permission to participate as a family in the worship this day, as greeters, as liturgists, or as servers of communion. If children of the Sunday school are not baking the communion BREAD, find out if your family might make it. The recipe you use must make a firm bread that is not crumbly. One recipe is included in the Sunday school section. Talk with children about the significance of bread and the nutrients it contains. Look up bread in a Bible CONCORDANCE and read verses in which it is mentioned. Read about bread as it appears in the words of the Lord's Prayer. Explain that in Jesus' land and time in history people were poor and often didn't know if they would have bread enough for the next day's meal.

Help children to deepen their understanding of communion by sharing its meaning and purpose in your lives with them. Attend WORSHIP services and take communion together as a family. Then go out and eat dinner in a RESTAURANT of an ethnic or nationality group that is different from your own to celebrate the wonderful diversity of peoples around the world.

HALLOWEEN OR
ALL HALLOWS' EVE

This holiday combines the ancient Roman festival of Pomona, the goddess of fruit, with Druidic beliefs and Christian superstitions. The use of nuts and apples dates back to the Roman observance.

In northern and western Europe (especially in Ireland and Scotland) the Celtic order of Druids celebrated the fall harvest with mystical ceremonies on October 31, the eve of Samhain or summer's end. The sun god was thanked for the harvest, and the summer food supplies were opened for a feast. Hearth fires were extinguished, and people gathered at a sacred altar to receive new fires ignited by the priests. Bonfires were also lit on hilltops to honor the sun god and to frighten away evil spirits. People then carried the sacred fires to relight their hearths, believing they would be protected from evil.

Many curious customs and superstitions developed around this holiday. For example, it was believed that the spirits of those who had died during the previous year returned to their homes for one last visit; so families wanting the departed to see that all was well would display around the kitchen food grown that year.

One superstition involved marking a white stone for each family member and dropping the stones into the fire. If any stone was missing the next morning, it served as a sign of death in the coming year for that family member.

A similar custom was carried out with nuts; if they burned well, prosperity would come to the owner; but when they smoldered and turned black, ill fortune awaited.

The early Christian church adopted the day and gave it the name of "All Hallows' Eve" or "All Saints' Eve," and, as with many other holidays, changed the celebration to be more in keeping with Christian Catholicism. Worship services, often held outside at midnight and including prayer for the souls of departed friends, were combined with setting large fires along hillsides. These fires, called "tindles," were jokingly explained as lighting souls out of purgatory.

In Spain, religious persons spent the evening in prayer, burning candles or oil lamps and often going to the cemetery or church to pray for the deceased.

As late as the nineteenth century in Ireland, Scotland, and Wales, Christians believed that restless spirits were out on this night stealing milk and creating mischief. This caused people to spend the night swapping ghost stories in the security of groups.

Spirits which abounded on this night were thought to be able to predict the future. Therefore cakes or colcannon (a dish of mashed potatoes, parsnips, and onions) were baked; and a ring, a thimble, small doll, and coin were stirred into it. The one who found the ring would marry, the doll symbolized having children, the thimble meant spinsterhood, and the person who received the coin would find wealth.

Jack o' lanterns originated from an Irish legend about a man named Jack, who was barred from heaven for his stinginess and also from hell because of his practical jokes on the devil. Thereafter he was doomed to wander the earth with his lantern until Judgment Day. Scottish children carved their lanterns from large turnips, since pumpkins didn't grow in their country.

Although the idea of witches originated outside the Christian church, belief in them persisted for many years within Christianity until the late 1700s. The witch trials of the early American colonies are well known.

Among some Christian groups today this holiday is regarded as a celebration that honors satanic forces and one which should be abandoned. Many have substituted "Harvest Festivals" and parties where children wear biblical costumes for traditional Halloween celebrations. It is important to remember that most of our religious holidays including Christmas (Dec. 25 was the birthday of the sun god) have pagan beginnings. Before discarding a special time, we need to look for new meanings and acceptable ways to enjoy it. Halloween, as celebrated today, with parties, costumes, and trick-or-treating (in "safe" settings) are mostly just fun. Certainly dressing up in costume and pretending to be someone different gives children an opportunity to use their imaginations.

October 31 is a day on which two other important events are celebrated. It is UNICEF Day because of a presidential proclamation in 1967. Trick or treating to obtain money for food and medicine for the world's children is certainly a worthy cause.

HALLOWEEN IN CHURCH SETTINGS

Since this holiday has minimal religious significance, it might not be appropriate to include it in the Sunday school experience unless you are collecting MONEY for UNICEF (United Nations International Children's Emergency Fund) or want to make hospital tray favors. The UNICEF office (US Committee for UNICEF, 331 E. 38th St., N.Y., NY 10016) will provide you with trick or TREAT BOXES and other information about this fund which you can share with children before having them collect the money.

Tray FAVORS may be made of cone-shaped construction paper, with Jack o' lanterns, owls, and witches on the top.

You may, however, decide to host a churchwide Halloween PARTY. Halloween night is the best night to do this since it keeps children off the streets and provides a safe environment for them.

Admission to the party might include a sack of wrapped candies or PRIZES, plus a small fee to cover the cost of refreshments and drinks. Candies and prizes will be handed out as children play games or trick or treat around the church grounds.

Adults and children alike may arrive dressed in costumes. If you prefer, costumes may be created by everyone during the party. Newspapers, large paper sacks, bits of ribbon, cloth, and other items from your church supply room can be used for this purpose. A costume PARADE with prizes for the funniest, most original, scariest, ugliest, and other categories can conclude this activity. It's important to affirm all children and give prizes to everyone.

A PUMPKIN CARVING contest can be held, either by bringing completed Jack o'lanterns from home or by carving them at the party.

Carnival booths make for a fun party. These might include a ball toss into a cardboard ghost with mouth opened wide, witches on a wooden tree that can be knocked down with bean bags made to look like frogs, pinning spiders on a web when blindfolded, and a candle squirt (candles set in sand or holders and using squirt guns to try to extinguish the flames). Scar or wound painting (use makeup or poster paints) and throwing wet sponges at a church member are other ideas. Treats should be given at each game regardless of who wins or loses.

Trick or treating in classrooms where adults or youth are dressed in costumes in decorated settings and perhaps some eerie music will add to the fun.

Ghost storytelling in a darkened room away from the rest of the

party is something children enjoy but needs to be limited to third grade and older. A sample story is included. For refreshments try

Witches' Brew

1	(16 oz.) can apple cider or juice	¼	tsp. nutmeg
2	tbl. brown sugar	1	stick cinnamon
		1	tsp. allspice

Heat and place in a kettle (cauldron). Put on a tray that has dry ice on it for a smokey appearance. Add black licorice sticks and doughnuts and a witch to serve it all.

Singing is always fun for everyone and a good way to end a party. Books of pumpkin carols can be purchased through Hallmark Stores under the title, *The Peanuts Book of Pumpkin Carols,* by United Feature Syndicate, Inc. They are excellent songs.

THE REMAINS OF GRAVEL GERDIE
by Judy Weaver

Zack was a skinny, spindly little man with wild wisps of hair sticking out of his head in all directions. "It's no wonder," the townspeople whispered, "with a wife like Gerdie." It was rumored she dragged the poor man around by his hair. Her voice, deep and penetrating and angry, caused her to be nicknamed "Gravel Gerdie," by everyone. She was often heard from morning until night taunting poor Zack. That is, she was heard until the night of the storm.

October 31st started out like many an autumn night. A soft drizzle descended on the valley, followed by thick bluish fog which covered everything. Later, the neighbors would admit to having heard low moans coming from old Zack's farm in the middle of the night, and finally one eery heart-rending. . . . . *(pause, and then scream in your loudest voice).* Then all was still.

The next day dawned cloudy and gray but not unlike many others, except that no one heard Gerdie's voice. A few days of quiet went by before someone finally had the courage to approach Zack and inquire about his wife.

"Oh, she's gone to visit a sister in Devonshire. Be gone a while, I imagine." He smiled an unnatural smile and went back to his haying.

It all seemed quite unlikely. No one had seen her leave, nor could anyone recall that she'd ever gone away before; but then people were mostly glad she wasn't around anymore.

Several months went by uneventfully until the night the dam broke. It was at the north side of town and hardly held enough water to matter. Besides, it hadn't even rained; but a mysterious hole appeared at its base, and all sorts of red mud and grit . . . *(pause)* and other things oozed out.

The townspeople hurried out to see it. The grocer found the first pieces of evidence. He picked up hard white pieces and passed them around the crowd. "Why, it's someone's teeth," he exclaimed. *(Pass around corn kernels or teeth from the dentist.)*

"I've something else," remarked a young boy. *(Pass around cooked spaghetti or cow's intestines.)* "I think it's guts!"

A couple of ears were passed around next *(pass dried pears or apricots)*, followed by brains *(a wet sponge or cow's brain)* and 2 beady eyes *(peeled grapes)* and a lock of gray hair *(yarn or piece of a wig)*.

All was quiet until a large icy hand was given to each to hold *(freeze water in a rubber glove and pass it around)*.

As everyone shivered, a deep gravel voice was heard to say, "You'll never get rid of me now. I'm unloosed from the dam and I'll invade each of your houses until you find all of my parts and lock them in a heavy vault *(pause, then laugh deeply and hysterically)*.

Halloween Get-Acquainted Game

1. Go up to someone and make a howl like a coyote.   They initial here _____.

2. Tell one person his/her costume looks great.   They initial here _____.

3. Walk up to a friend and exchange loud, long boo's.   They initial here _____.

4. Back up to 2 people and make a noise like a squeeking door.   Initials_____.

5. Pretend to be a black cat and give a loud cry and show your claws at the person closest to you.   Initials_____.

6. Say "Trick or treat!" to everyone you meet until one person gives you something.

7. Go up to someone and say,   Initials_____.
   "I just saw a ghost!" in as
   scary a voice as you can
   muster.
8. Show one person your face   Initials_____.
   like Dracula with fangs.
9. Walk up to a person of the   Initials_____.
   opposite sex and pretend to
   be a witch on a broomstick.
10. Cackle or laugh in a   Initials_____.
    mischievous way to
    someone across the room.

HALLOWEEN IN FAMILY SETTINGS

This holiday lends itself to exciting family interaction and enjoyment, so join right in and all play together.

Shopping for a pumpkin (or several) to carve is an adventure which all members can share. If you live near a pumpkin field, that is even better. Growing your own pumpkins is another good idea. They require little care and produce well.

PUMPKIN FACES may be painted with poster paints, or carved, or decorated in a variety of unusual ways. Vegetables can be used in the decorating, with potatoes for ears, carrot noses, carrot stalks for hair, yellow squash for a funny hat. Add your own ideas. Glasses can be made of construction paper to create quite a funny face.

Keep the seeds—they may be roasted and eaten later.

Pumpkin Seeds

1 c. seeds (cleaned)   1 tsp. salt or garlic salt or
1 tbl. melted butter   seasoned salt

Spread thinly on a baking sheet with butter and salt of your choice. Bake at 300° approximately 30 minutes, stirring and turning them once. Eat when they have become crisp and have turned slightly brown.

You might also DECORATE your home for Halloween. Cobwebs can be made from cotton batting and draped over lamps, pictures, and the fireplace.

A CORNSTALK scarecrow made from old trousers and workshirt and stuffed with newspapers or corn husks can be set outside your front door. The face can be hidden with a big old hat.

One family in my neighborhood creates a ghostly scene in their diningroom by dressing MANNEQUINS in old-fashioned clothes and ugly masks and sitting or standing them around the table. An eerie orange light burns instead of the usual light, and cobwebs are visible around the room.

LUMINARIAS can line your front walk. Use white or orange lunch sacks; let children cut out black cats and orange Jack o' lanterns and glue them on the front and back of the sacks. Place about 1½ inches of sand in the bottom of each sack with a votive candle in the middle of the sand. Once it gets dark and these are lit, they will give a festive glow to any walkway.

A family fun Halloween DINNER can begin with a small plastic Jack o' lantern at each plate filled with candy—or by carving out the insides of an orange, painting a face on the outside, filling with treats, and replacing the lid. The menu might include:

Orange Chicken

Cut up pieces of chicken (approximately 3 lb. with skin removed)

½	c. butter	½	tsp. ginger
¼	c. flour	2	c. orange juice
½	tsp. salt	¼	tsp. pepper
2	tbl. brown sugar		

Brown the chicken in ¼ cup of butter in a hot frying pan. Remove it from the pan. Melt the remaining butter and stir all of the above ingredients in a *clean* pan. Then place the chicken and ingredients into a baking dish. Cover and bake for 30 minutes at 350° or until done. Add extra orange juice if it becomes dry. (Recipe may also be cooked in an electric frypan.) Turn the meat occasionally and baste with the juices.

When the chicken is nearly done, add one 18 oz. can of sweet potatoes and one large navel orange sliced into circles, arranging the oranges around the top. Allow this to bake 15 minutes longer. It's delicious and attractive too.

Colcannon is an old-fashioned potato dish designed for Halloween. Try it!

Colcannon

1 head of cabbage	¼ c. margarine or butter
1 c. water	1½ tsp. salt
4 c. mashed potatoes	¼ tsp. nutmeg
½ c. finely chopped onions	½ tsp. pepper
¼ c. heavy cream	

Shred the cabbage until you have 8 cups. Cook until done in salted water. Drain well, add mashed potatoes, onions, cream, margarine, salt, pepper, and nutmeg. (You might also add 1½ to 2 cups of grated cheese and might substitute 3 cups of chopped cooked parsnips for the cabbage.) Put it into a baking dish; add dabs of butter and a sprinkle of additional nutmeg. Then, drop a few small coins in the mixture and bake at 350° for 20 to 30 minutes. Serve warm. The persons who receive a coin may make a special wish for themselves or the family.

If your church or community does not have Halloween parties, you might like to have one for your neighborhood by using the ideas listed under the church Halloween party.

Reformation Day

Martin Luther was born in Eisleben, Saxony, on November 10, 1483, to a family of poor peasants. But Martin received a good education, including a university degree at Erfurt, then a master's degree. Finally, he began to study law. A violent thunderstorm changed the direction of his life. When lightning threw him to the ground, he vowed to St. Anne to become a monk if he were only saved from the storm's fury.

Martin proved to be a monk of the strictest discipline and took seriously the vows of poverty, obedience, and chastity. He received further education in theology at the University of Erfurt. Soon he became a teacher of Bible at Wittenburg University, where he experienced a conflict in his faith. He had joined a religious order in search of his own salvation by a merciful God but was scandalized by the luxurious and licentious lives of some of the priests. The teachings of salvation by works especially troubled him, as did the purchasing of indulgences which were being urged by Pope Leo X and promoted by Johann Tetzel, the Pope's chief agent. An indulgence was the means by which souls were saved from purgatory when relatives paid money to release them. Luther was convinced that this practice was demoralizing and crooked.

In response to these troubling practices, Luther wrote a thesis of 95 points and nailed it on the door of Wittenburg Church on October 31, 1517. Though it was written in Latin, German translations were available very quickly. The people of his country supported him enthusiastically.

The Pope ordered Martin Luther to recant; he refused and instead gave public speeches supporting his viewpoint. He became convinced that salvation was achieved by faith (not works), that the Bible was the only true authority to reveal God, and that the papacy was the work of the devil. He further promoted the priesthood of all believers and challenged the church's rules about fasting, masses, holidays, and celibacy of the priesthood.

At a hearing before the Emperor Charles V, Luther is said to have restated his beliefs and ended by saying, "Here I stand, I can do no other. God help me. Amen." These words stand as a symbol of his defiance and of his faith. He was to spend some time in hiding, protected by friends, before finally being excommunicated by the

Roman Catholic Church. During this period he wrote several books and began his famous translation of the Bible into German.

On June 13, 1525, Martin married a former nun, Catherine Von Bora. They had six children and, along with several nieces and nephews who lived with them, formed a very large family. Students enjoyed being entertained by the Luthers. The many conversations in their home were written down and later published as "Table Talk."

Though other groups were also straining against the restrictions of Catholicism and establishing their own religious denominations, Martin Luther is considered the outstanding leader of the Reformation movement. It is he who is remembered on this important Sunday.

Though it was not his intention to form a new church, only to reform an old one, Lutheranism became strong not only in Germany but in many other European countries, including Scandinavia. It was introduced in America by many immigrants from these lands.

Historically this day has been celebrated by singing "A Mighty Fortress Is Our God," a hymn written by Luther. A favorite scripture is John 2:13-17, the story of Jesus driving out the moneychangers in the temple. This is certainly a good example of Christ's attempt to reform Judaism. Previously it was traditional to act out skits depicting this great reformer, but Vatican II in the Roman Catholic Church has brought about significant internal changes. Thus many churches today view Reformation Day as a time to continue to examine and improve upon the direction of their own church, whatever the denomination.

Roman Catholic theologians who once considered Luther a heretic have now come to adopt some of Luther's ideas, to reappraise how they view him, and even to participate in combined interdenominational services celebrating his life.

REFORMATION SUNDAY
IN SUNDAY SCHOOL SETTINGS

On this day ask children to name as many different Christian denominations as they can. List them on the chalkboard. Ask children why they think there are so many groups. Share names and stories of some of the great reformers (Calvin, Wesley, Booth, Otterbein, and Luther—to name a few). Stress that each leader wanted to improve a denomination but ended by forming a new one instead. Share conversation about how difficult change is for all of us, how cemented we become to our own ideas, and how resistant we are to hearing and accepting a new idea.

Share the scripture example in which Jesus attempted to reform Jewish practices with which he disagreed. Try a short SKIT: Act out the story of Jesus overturning the tables in the temple (John 2:13-17). Point out that in other versions of this story, Jesus performs this act at the end of his ministry instead of the beginning. Speculate for a few minutes about this difference.

Plan a TABLEAU or human, still-life picture depicting six or seven of the greatest religious reformers. Costumes can be created for each reformer. Choose a narrator and write a few appropriate sentences for each leader. In a tableau, a large picture frame forms the picture. At an appropriate moment each child steps into it, posing as in a photograph and remaining perfectly still until the narration is completed, and then stepping out for the next figure. If planned and rehearsed ahead of time, this may be presented to parents at a special program.

Several children might read parts of Martin Luther's 95 point thesis, which is re-written into their language. The program could conclude with the CAROLS, "Away in a Manger" (traditionally associated with Luther) and "A Mighty Fortress Is Our God."

On this Sunday, children might also list some ways in which they think that Christians today need to improve their lives. Describe how each person can do this at school, home, and play.

An appropriate activity might be to make cardboard cross NECK-LACES. The cross would be sprayed with gold paint and attached to a gold cord. By wearing these crosses, the children will remember Martin Luther, the monk who became a reformer.

REFORMATION SUNDAY IN FAMILY SETTINGS

A conversation about the Lutheran and Roman Catholic Churches is a good way to introduce this day. The family might enjoy visiting both types to compare ways in which they are alike and different. Actually similarities today are much more noticeable than the differences which arose in Martin Luther's time. An alternate idea is to visit a monastery, priory, or (for Californians and Southwesterners) a mission. The purpose for these activities is to promote understanding as well as to recognize that different groups of people experience God in ways which are meaningful for them.

Luther strongly believed that scripture was the primary way in which we come to know God. In addition he believed that the Bible should be available for all people to read for themselves. Thus an appropriate food for this day is a SCRIPTURE CAKE. The Revised Standard Version will be needed for each assistant cook. If you should run into difficulty when translating scripture into ingredients, clues may be found below in the instructions for preparation.

Scripture Cake

¾ c. soft Psalm 55:21
1½ c. Jeremiah 6:20
4 Isaiah 10:14, separated
3 c. sifted Leviticus 24:5
¾ tsp. 2 Kings 2:20
3 tsp. Amos 4:5
1 tsp. Exodus 30:23 (2nd spice)

¼ tsp. each 2 Chronicles 9:9
   (see clue below)
⅔ c. Exodus 19b
¾ c. chopped Genesis 43:11
   (next to last noun)
¾ c. 2 Samuel 16:1
¾ c. slivered Genesis 43:11 (last word)

Cream shortening and sugar; add egg yolks. Beat egg whites until foamy. Beat into first mixture sifted flour, salt, baking powder, cinnamon, cloves, allspice, and nutmeg. Add milk and beaten egg whites. Lastly add chopped nuts, figs, and raisins and bake in a 9" x 13" pan at 325° approximately 50 minutes or until done. Frost with a cream cheese icing and top with slivered almonds.

ALL SAINTS' DAY AND
ALL SOULS' DAY

NOVEMBER 1 AND 2

As with many Christian holidays, these two days have pagan origins. They began as a time when the Druids celebrated the fall festival by sacrificing a horse to the sun god. On the eve of All Souls', fires were extinguished except for the sacred fire from which people relighted their homes. Fruit and grain offerings were made to the Lord of Death who judged souls and decided on people's punishment or reward in the afterlife. Peasants often spent the night in prayers for loved ones.

Then in 609 Pope Boniface III rededicated the Parthenon in Rome (a center of Roman mythology) to the virgin Mary and all martyrs (saints). In an attempt to rid the church of pagan celebrations, he declared a date in May for this event.

While November first was generally recognized as a day for all saints, All Souls' Day was declared a time of special observance for all the faithful departed who were not elevated to sainthood and as a day of intercession on behalf of souls locked in purgatory.

Many countries established customs around this holiday. In Austria peasants believed that, if you visited the cemetery on the eve of All Souls', you would see a procession of the dead followed by those who would die in the coming year. Based on this story a play, "The Miller and His Daughter," is acted out each year in Vienna. In the play, the lover visits the cemetery only to discover that he and the miller will die soon.

It was also on this evening in parts of Great Britain that bonfires and bundles of lighted straw were tossed into the air, representing souls escaping from purgatory. Along with this ritual, short prayers for the dead were offered.

Throughout Roman Catholic countries in Europe and Latin America today, this holiday is observed in churches with flowers, lighted candles, and joyful music to honor the saints. People decorate cemeteries and stores and sell colorful wreaths and flowers for this purpose. In Alpine villages, women weave wreaths of evergreens and flowers and carry them to graves along with lighted lamps, giving cemeteries a gala appearance.

Since the Reformation, this holiday has lost much of its significance because many Protestant churches no longer regard it as important.

However, in some, most notably the Anglican church, it is still observed; and the Common Book of Prayer contains a ritual for this day.

Some Protestant denominations, such as United Methodists, often observe All Saints' Day (but not All Souls' Day) in worship by singing hymns such as "For All the Saints" and by reading the names of church members who have died in the preceding twelve months. These names are often listed in the Sunday bulletin as well.

Special significance can be added to this day by involving children in worship, each dressed to represent important Christians who might be regarded as "saints" both present and past. Costumes can be quite simple: for example, Dr. Albert Schweitzer dressed in a white shirt and trousers with a toy stethoscope. Each child should carry the name of his or her saint written in large print on a card. Children will then process into the sanctuary one at a time as someone from the lectern shares the name and a short sentence about this person. One or more children in the procession might represent special members of your congregation whom you regard as saints because of all their service to the church and the community.

Possible "saints" and words that might be used to describe them:

1. Frances Asbury was the first Methodist Bishop in the American colonies.
2. Clara Barton founded the American Red Cross.
3. John Calvin was a church reformer and founder of the Presbyterian church.
4. Fanny Crosby was a hymn writer, author of "Jesus Is Tenderly Calling."
5. Tom Dooley was a doctor who cared for the sick in Vietnam and who died there of cancer.
6. Victor Frankl, theologian and scholar, spent World War II in a prison camp. He wrote about his strong faith in God.
7. William Booth, Methodist pastor, founded the Salvation Army.
8. Johann Gutenberg, inventor of the printing press, printed the Bible, making it available to everyone.
9. Dag Hammersköld, Swedish Secretary General of the United Nations, had strong views on world peace and was killed in an airplane crash.
10. Helen Keller, though blind and deaf after having measles at

age two, became a writer and impressive speaker about her
religious faith.

11. Martin Luther King, Jr., a black Baptist minister, believed in
nonviolence and spoke for minority rights. He often was
imprisoned for his beliefs and finally was assassinated.

12. Martin Luther, a Roman Catholic monk, tried to reform his
church, founded the Lutheran Church, and became the
leader of the Protestant Reformation.

13. Mother Teresa, a Roman Catholic nun, is a missionary to the
very poorest people of India and the winner of many awards
for ministry and service.

14. Florence Nightingale, known as the lady with the lamp, was
the founder of modern nursing.

15. Philip Otterbein was a German preacher and founder of the
Evangelical Church which later merged with the United
Brethren and then the Methodist Church.

16. Harriet Tubman, a courageous black woman, helped slaves
escape through the underground railroad.

17. John Wesley, a Church of England preacher, became the
founder of Methodism.

18. Susannah Wesley, called the Mother of Methodism, bore 19
children (including John and Charles) and had a strong influence on her children. She also conducted Sunday school in
her home.

Many other names, including biblical characters, religious and
political leaders of your community, and members of your congregation, may be added to this list.

Scripture readings which can be used with this celebration are
Matthew 22:1-14, Matthew 23:1-12, Isaiah 26:1-4, 8-9, 12-13,
Psalm 149:1-5, and Matthew 5:1-12.

ALL SAINTS' DAY
IN SUNDAY SCHOOL SETTINGS

Prepare your classroom before children arrive by placing pictures,
stories, books, and names of special people who might be called
saints, around the classroom. They may be on bulletin boards, in the
story corner, on tables, cupboards, and in every corner of the room.

As children arrive, give each one paper and pencil. Ask them to walk around the room and write down as many NAMES OF SAINTS as they can find. Allow about fifteen minutes for this activity; then gather everyone together and see which person has the longest list.

Ask them if they know why these names are special, and then hold a discussion of people whom we might call "saints." Define saint as an ordinary person who, because of deep religious conviction, is able to live and do extraordinary things in the name of Christ.

Allow children to develop an additional list of special people they know who could be called saints. The list could include friends, relatives, and church members.

The children could research some of these names and give reports on different saints. This might be in the form of a role play or TV news reporter interview. Each child would become his or her saint, dressed in appropriate costume. Microphones that actually work can be purchased in many toy stores and make good props (even without the batteries). The news reporter would ask them questions about who they are and in what way they have spent their life. Call letters of a local station might be used by the reporter. The class might even write up a series of "Christian commercials," calling persons to follow Christ.

The class might also read the BEATITUDES, study what each one means, and rewrite them in their own words or make up a list of beatitudes to be followed by anyone wishing to become a saint.

Your judicatory (or area) film and video library has many resources on special Christians. Call them to reserve a film for class.

Once children are somewhat familiar with saints, a game can be played. Put names on the children's backs and have them guess which saint's name they have. They can ask only questions which may be answered by yes or no. All other answers are forbidden. Play the game until all children have guessed the name they have.

A scavenger hunt for saints might be conducted by giving children a list of people whose names they are to find.

Scavenger Hunt List
  1. Find the name of a church secretary who gives many hours each week in service to God and the church. _____

2. In *(name a location)* you will find a photograph of the founder of Anglicanism, Methodism, Lutherans, etc. Who is he?____
3. The choir room has a name of a special writer of Christian music. Who is this person?_____
4. On the door of the pastor's office is a name of a special saint for God. Write it here. _____
5. In the Fellowship Hall is a plaque which dedicates the room to the memory of a special church member. List it here. _____

The list can go on and on and must fit your special church facility and family. Have a conversation about ways we can be saints today and as we grow up. List children's ideas on the board. As they leave class give each child a wrapped gift box with instructions not to open it until they arrive home. On the outside of the box write the words "saint of the Christian church." Inside place a small mirror.

CELEBRATING ALL SAINTS' DAY
IN FAMILY SETTINGS

On this day, talk in your family about special Christians who have enriched your lives. They might be family members, Sunday school teachers, persons out of your past, or those you know in the church today. Adults as well as children need to share in the conversation, and persons of any age can be a saint. Develop a list of persons who are important. Then, in a few moments of worship time together, recall them, thanking God for their lives.

Read the BEATITUDES (Matthew 5:1-11) all together and discuss them. Other Beatitudes can be found in Matthew 11:6, Matthew 13:16, Matthew 24:46, Luke 6:17-49, Luke 11:28, Luke 14:13-14, and John 20:29.

Another scripture reading of importance at this time is Matthew 25:31-45. It tells about feeding the hungry, welcoming the stranger, clothing the naked, and caring for those who are sick or imprisoned. Share with children that many people who have been listed as saints have followed these verses, making it their ministry to fulfill the words in this scripture. You might talk about Christians who have done this. Your church or public library will have information about them which you may obtain.

As a family decide what you can do to help others in light of this scripture.

Each family member might ADOPT A SPECIAL SAINT whom they want to emulate after doing special research on this person.

If deceased family members are buried in cemeteries close by your home, you might visit them and talk further with children about them. It's important that children know their family's history. You might also share some of the history of Halloween or All Hallows' Eve and All Saints' Day as shared earlier to help them understand this holy day.

If your church doesn't have a special All Saints' Day service, visit one that does. A Roman Catholic church in your town or city is certain to do so.

One last family idea is to rent a VIDEOTAPE about someone whose life has been special and view it together. There are many excellent movies which highlight the lives of special persons and ministries. If your local video store doesn't carry them, Ecufilm (1-800-251-4091; Tennessee 615-242-6277) probably does.

Share popcorn and cider together as you do this.

Spicy Popcorn

3 qts. popped unsalted popcorn	½ c. melted butter or oleo
1 c. nuts (peanuts or other kind)	1 pkge. taco seasoning mix
	¼ c. brown sugar

Stir one package of taco seasoning mix and ¼ cup brown sugar together. Mix all ingredients with the popcorn and bake at 300°, 8-10 minutes, being careful it doesn't burn.

THANKSGIVING FOURTH THURSDAY IN NOVEMBER

This is the only nationally celebrated holiday whose date each year is set by presidential proclamation. Thanksgiving has a long and surprising history which dates back to biblical times where the celebration of Succoth (Tabernacle) was observed five days following Yom Kippur, the Day of Atonement.

Though the pilgrims are credited with the first American Thanksgiving, its history here dates back to 1578 when an English minister named Wolfall conducted a worship service of Thanksgiving on the shores of New Foundland after accompanying the first English Colony to the new world.

The first official day of Thanksgiving, however, was proclaimed by Governor Bradford on December 13, 1621. It was to be a day of feasting the thanksgiving. Men were sent out to hunt for game and returned with wild fowl (principally turkeys). They had enough to feed the colony for a week, and women prepared all else that was needed for the mealtimes.

A cannon's blast was the call to worship. A dinner feast followed. Ten Native Americans of the nearby tribe, led by King Massasoit, joined in the party. They arrived bearing huge haunches of venison. It seems they were not actually invited, although it was indeed appropriate for the pilgrims to celebrate with the tribe that helped them survive during that first year in a new land. Half the colony had died from cold and disease. Growing food in the rocky New England soil was not an easy task and the Native Americans had provided both skill and seeds needed by the pilgrims.

This Thanksgiving celebration lasted for three days and included singing of songs, dances by the Native Americans, and exhibitions of military skill by Captain Standish's men.

In succeeding years, Thanksgiving was celebrated only when people felt they had a reason to do so. A successful year or military victory over the natives gave them cause to celebrate.

Beginning in 1684, it became an annual event in the Massachusetts Colony; and in a few years, all of New England joined in the celebration.

During the Revolutionary War, Thanksgiving celebrations were spread among the soldiers who were fighting. At Valley Forge, Washington declared December 18, 1777, as a day of general thanksgiving.

Later when he became president, he named Thursday, November 26, as the special time for this holiday.

Southern states, especially during the Civil War, disregarded the day since they associated it with the Puritans and thought it was their substitute for Christmas (a forbidden holiday of this somber group).

Finally, Mrs. Sarah Hale succeeded in having the fourth Thursday of November declared the official Thanksgiving Day.

Early Thanksgivings were often accompanied by hunting expeditions and raffles (chances sold on game). These were held on Thanksgiving Eve. Shooting matches, held the next morning, allowed the men to avoid attending worship in the churches.

Throughout our history, Thanksgiving Day sermons have leaned toward secular topics, such as local and national patriotism; but Thanksgiving has also been a time to thank God for the good things of the preceding year. It is always a holiday of great feasting and a time for reunion of family and friends. Traditional foods of the day continue to be those introduced by the Native Americans of Massachusetts: turkey, dressing, squash, pumpkin, cranberries, yams, and Indian pudding are among those special dishes.

Many churches either conduct their own worship services or combine with nearby congregations for community services. Hymns such as "Come, Ye Thankful People, Come" and other harvest songs are popular. Sunday school classes often build *succoth* (booths) for patio, altar area, or narthex in remembrance of the biblical harvest roots of this day; and canned foods for the hungry are placed inside the booth.

The place of the Native Americans in this holiday is now ignored or relegated to school plays which usually depict inaccurate images of the contribution made by King Massasoit and his men. What began as an act of kindness and friendship on the part of these people was quickly turned into hatred and fighting as the colonists demanded more and more land and drove out the Indians. The white people forgot that Jesus said to love your neighbor as yourself or the example of kindness given in Jesus' story of the good Samaritan. On this day, it is appropriate to pause and remember the contribution of this great group of people. If your church is near a Native American congregation, a combined service of worship would be an excellent way to recreate the roots of this day. For other churches, a Thanksgiving dinner for members, friends, and those who are alone might be appropriate. In one area of California, a district superintendent's family offers dinner in a park, with churches purchasing blocks of tickets to be given to members of its congregation who desire a place in which to celebrate this holiday. This indeed gives the day extra meaning for workers and participants.

CELEBRATING THANKSGIVING IN SUNDAY SCHOOL SETTINGS

The children's curriculum generally tells the story of Hebrew Thanksgiving traditions as found in Leviticus 23:33-43 and suggests that classes build *succoth*, the Hebrew word for booths. However a different emphasis for the class would be to delve into the American roots of the holiday and share the story of pilgrims and Native Americans. Although this is taught in school, special emphasis might be given to the religious convictions of the pilgrims and how all of us need to follow our beliefs. Consider also the kindness of the Indians in assisting their new neighbors. Share the good Samaritan story to emphasize this point. A further explanation of the ways Native people have been misrepresented in American history (and films) should be given. It is important for us to remember that the Europeans, not the natives, were intruders. Today most Indians prefer to be called Native Americans in recognition of this fact.

From a church or city video library rent a film or filmstrip of Indian legends or read a book of Indian tales. Call attention to words used for God (Great Spirit, Shepherd Chief, etc.) and together write a prayer of Thanksgiving, using an Indian style of language.

Special Bible verses can also be used from the Psalms, especially Psalms 67, 95, 96, 98, and 100. After reading one psalm, think about it from the Native American perspective by considering the reverence and respect that they have for all of God's creation— earth, sky, seas, and all other living creatures. Perhaps the class could write their own POEM with this in mind.

Psalms might also be painted, with each child doing one verse. PICTURES can then be mounted, arranged in order, and displayed in the church social hall or other special location. Take slides of the artwork and share later with parents or other Sunday school classes.

Pilgrim Boy's Hat

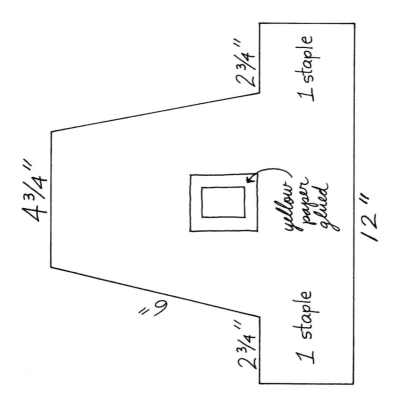

Measure child's head and then staple a strip of paper to the hat and around the child's head.

Pilgrim Girl's Hat

Fold hat back on dotted line. Staple point A to point A and point B to point B.

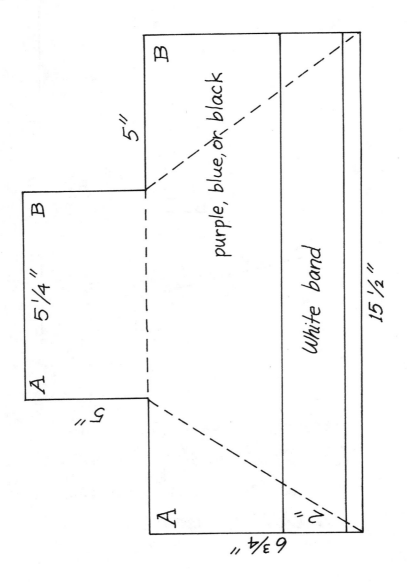

Another idea for this holiday is to have several Sunday school classes share in writing a booklet of PRAYERS. It could be titled "Prayers to Pray at Thanksgiving." These might be gathered from adults as well and distributed to the congregation.

Choose a special Saturday and have an EARLY AMERICAN DAY. Allow the children to dress in costumes and move around the classroom doing activities that would have been common to life in the colonies. These might include grinding wheat with a mortar and pestle, making homemade butter by shaking cream in a glass jar, attempting to knit (a church member who does this could share), candle making (melt down old candles and remold in a juice can), and other activities.

Indian fry bread is fun to make and really delicious to eat.

Fry Bread

3	cups flour	6	tbl. powdered milk
1½	tsp. shortening	1½	tsp. salt

Combine all ingredients, add lukewarm water (small amount at a time) until a soft-but-not-sticky dough is formed. Take a handful of dough and pat it with your hands, stretching it until it is about ¼" thick (or roll it out with a rolling pin). Fry it in a large frying pan in hot grease 1½" deep. It should spread out in the pan. Brown it on both sides and serve warm with honey and powdered sugar or add fried ground beef, chopped lettuce, tomatoes, grated cheese, and chopped onion for a lunch treat.

Make apple sauce to eat along with the fry bread. Peel and cut apples and heat them with a small amount of water in a saucepan. (This may be cooked over a hot plate.) It is not necessary to add sugar, as apples are already sweet without it. Mash the apples as they are softening until all lumps are removed. Add a few raisins and cook until soft to give it special flavor.

PLACEMATS can be made for lunch or snack time by tracing leaves (oak or maple have the prettiest shapes), cutting them out in bright fall colors, and glueing them onto construction paper 12" x 18" size. A cut-out pumpkin and prayer can be added. Clear contact paper will make it washable and more durable.

Napkin rings can be made with paper towel rolls. Cut out circles approximately 1½" wide. Cover with foil or patterned contact paper. Glue a leaf or pumpkin cutout alongside each napkin ring. Children might make extras of these to take home.

Tray FAVORS for hospital or nursing home are always welcome. Here's one to try:

Thanksgiving Turkeys

2 prunes or 2 dates   4 or 5 raisins
3 toothpicks   1 small feather
1 piece of pimento

Break 2 toothpicks to approximately 2" in length, insert into the center of one prune (or date) to form legs. Set them in the remaining prune so they will stand. Break the remaining toothpick into 2" size. This is the neck. Insert into top and at one end of the prune. Cover it with raisins and the pimento to form the neck, wattles, and head. Poke a small feather into the back to make a tail. These are fast and easy to make.

One further idea is for a class to write their own Thanksgiving WORSHIP service. Two Sundays will be needed plus copies of the worship bulletin for each child. The different parts of the service need to be pointed out and explained. When they are ready, children can write their own order of worship following this format. (See *Helping Children Feel at Home in Church,* by Margie Morris, for more information on the order of worship. Available from Discipleship Resources, order no. DRO54B.) Select children to be acolytes, ushers, liturgist, and preacher. (One child can write a sermon, or a message can be read from lessons in the curriculum.) Bulletins need to be typed, including names of children taking "parts" in the worship. A children's announcement section is also a good idea.

The following Sunday, arrange the classroom to match your SANC-TUARY. Add flowers, cross, and offering plates to the altar. Conduct worship as you have designed it, keeping in mind that though this is a good learning experience, it is more of a role play than a worship time for children.

CELEBRATING THANKSGIVING
IN FAMILY SETTINGS

Our family has had a tradition of inviting special GUESTS to celebrate this day. Sometimes it's a person who needs a "family" for a day, someone who is far from home, but it might be a neighbor or church member. As a family, this year consider whom you might invite to share this special holiday.

During the weeks before thanksgiving, talk with your children of the history of this day; share the life and culture of early pioneers and of the Native American. If your family is not in a rural setting where farming is a fact of life, you might wish to talk also about the growing and harvesting of crops and the kind of work and commitment that is involved.

An activity for the family might be DYING a piece of white CLOTH using a natural dye made from flowers or beet juice. Extract the color from the water after boiling the vegetable or flower. Drain the water into another container and place the cloth in it. Allow it to sit there until the desired color has been achieved. Remove cloth and allow it to dry in the air.

Instead of eating your usual Thanksgiving dessert, try the following recipe.

Indian Pudding

Scald 4 cups of milk; add ½ tsp. salt. Moisten 7 tbs. cornmeal with a small amount of milk and then stir it into the hot milk. Add ¾ cup molasses and 2 tbl. butter. Add 1 tsp. cinnamon, and dash of cloves.
Pour into a baking dish and bake at 300° to 325°, 3 to 4 hours until firm. Serve with brown sugar and cream.

Play a game with your guests. Try to remember the names of as many groups of Native Americans as possible. While there are 10 different language groups of Indians in the United States, there are over 200 tribes. Not all of these are recognized by the government, and some of these are extinct. Give a prize to the guest who can get the most correct answers.

Using a map of the United States, make a list of as many Native American words as you can find that have become NAMES of cities, states, rivers, and lakes. You may be surprised at how many can be discovered.

Last, take time to share and be grateful for the wonderful blessings which you as a family (and gathered guests) have.

No one knows the exact date of Jesus' birth, but the date is not really important. However, setting aside a time to reflect on and celebrate this event is important. It is a fact that the pre-Christian roots of this holiday can be found in the pagan celebrations of many cultures. The Persian cult of Mithras (similar to Christianity in its celebration of baptism, the Sabbath, and a sacramental meal) celebrated the birth of their god on December 25. In the Roman Empire, Saturn was the god of farming. His special day, Saturnalia, was celebrated for seven days as a winter solstice ending in New Year celebrations honoring the deity, Janus. The Egyptians held a celebration of the sun on December 24, and they likened it to a newborn babe. Vikings, too, worshiped the sun on the shortest day of the year and lit huge bonfires in an effort to encourage its rebirth to lighten and warm the earth.

It is believed that early Christians began their celebration of Jesus' birth at this time of year in an effort to diminish pagan holidays and bring new meaning to the date. Pope Julius (A.D. 337 to 352), after some thoughtful research, officially declared December 25 as Jesus' birthday. While to many this holiday appears too secular and too commercial, it has indeed always been this way. Long ago people held raucous parties, ate huge banquets of food, and gave gifts on this date. The Romans exchanged dolls during Saturnalia.

Today many of our Christmas customs are a mixture of the pagan and some original Christian ideas. The yule log, now seldom used, can be traced back to the nativity of the sun and burning of bonfires. Another adaptation of pagan fire celebrations survives in candlelight services on Christmas eve and lights on the Christmas tree.

Mistletoe, found in homes but never in churches, is a survivor of Druidic customs where it was used to drive out the devils. It was also fed to cattle to cure them of ills, because farmers thought it held healing powers. Greenery and holly were chosen for decoration to show life and fertility in spite of winter's cold.

Though the person generally credited with the Christmas tree is Martin Luther, it was used earlier, during the Middle Ages, in a celebration of Adam and Eve. At that time it was adorned with fruit. Later candies, cookies, and other foods were added. Martin Luther is the one who brought the tree into the house and added lights to it. Candles on the tree were popular for many years, but buckets of water had to be placed nearby to extinguish any fires. Electricity made tree decorating much safer. Tree removal day was a joyous one as children could finally eat the good things which had adorned the tree.

The Christmas crèche, exchanging of greeting cards, and singing of carols are distinctly Christian additions to this holiday. Because boisterous parties and overindulgence in food and drink were also common, it is no wonder that the Puritans banned its celebration altogether, bringing this restriction with them to the new world. Governor Bradford considered it a workday but allowed persons who wished time off to rest, reflect, and pray in their homes. However, merrymaking in the streets and even games played with children were strictly forbidden.

When the English Parliament banned Christmas in 1659, Massachusetts Colony officially declared it a workday and banned any kind of celebration. Those who disobeyed the ruling were fined. A few years later, these laws were repealed; and Christmas regained both its religious and secular customs. In the midst of ever-growing commercialization, churches and families struggle to make Christmas a holy time.

CHRISTMAS IN CHURCH AND SUNDAY SCHOOL SETTINGS

There are countless ways churches can make the birthday of the Christchild more meaningful for families. The Christmas PAGEANT held in many churches is a valuable experience as children reenact the birth story, though it undoubtedly lacks perfection and creativity. *The Best Christmas Pageant Ever,* by Barbara Robinson, is a humorous story which is probably typical of actual pageants. In some churches, the hanging of the greens ceremony has developed into a singing extravaganza with the choir leading the congregation in a festive, musical sharing time.

An Alternative Christmas Sunday with BOOTHS representing specific projects to which people might contribute (in the name of a relative or friend) is a good way to de-emphasize materialism and focus on ways to help others. For more information write to Alternative Christmas, P.O. Box 429, Ellenwood, Georgia 30049.

Churches might prepare a daily Advent devotional BOOKLET by assigning a different scripture reference to each person, then asking them to add their thoughts for the season and a prayer for the day. The booklet might also include personal remembrances of Christmases past.

Greeting CARDS that feature a view of the sanctuary might be sold to the congregation. Drawings done by children make very appealing cards also. Should this become a project for your church, a day in late summer needs to be selected as a "Christmas Workshop" day. It should begin with the telling of the Christmas Story or a film about it. Various types of art materials can then be introduced: sponge paint, brush painting, use of marking pen, tissue paper art, and others. Allow children to participate in a variety of art projects, but emphasize that only artwork which depicts a religious aspect of Christmas will be entered into the contest. Pictures to be considered must also be easy to reproduce. A panel of judges can decide which picture best represents the church. An appropriate verse or greeting needs to be selected, and the winning child's name and the name of the church printed on the back of the card. Printing costs vary but generally escalate for every color on the card, so it is best to limit colors to no more than two or three. It also takes approximately three to four weeks for most printers to complete cards, so time needs to be allotted for this.

The Sunday when the cards are completed is a time to honor the artist with a small gift, a free box of cards, and recognition by the congregation. This is also the kick-off for card sales.

Your church might wish to contact the local cable TELEVISION station and inquire about air time during Advent, perhaps to close off the broadcast week on each Sunday evening with an Advent wreath worship ceremony presented by members of the congregation. This will give the community an opportunity to see the church since men, women, and children can participate in the taping. Some cable stations might require a team of three to six persons to attend the cable class and become the technical crew in order to film. However the experience will enable the church to use the studio and equipment for other taping sessions, perhaps establishing a regular taping schedule. Many stations provide this service, including air time, free of charge. Some stations do charge a small fee.

A Christmas family workshop held early in December is another idea that many churches pursue. At some WORKSHOPS, elaborate Advent wreaths can be made for home use while other workshops will offer varieties of decorations and gift-making activities. This offers children, youth, and adults opportunities to build and create gifts inexpensively and detract from the commercialization of Christmas. If you decide to have a workshop, various classrooms will be needed for the activities.

A staff of workers can each bring their ideas for the workshop. Magazines and craft books provide many possibilities. Woodworking projects are popular and look nice when completed, but activities such as cookie decorating and gingerbread house building are also fun.

In deciding on activities, the age range of the congregation should be considered so that there is something for everyone to do. At least one project should have some religious significance to it.

A simple but attractive CRÈCHE can be made with a 5″ x 4″ piece of very thin wood, 3 dowels ⅛″ in diameter, one dowel 2½″ long, and the other two 2″ long. Glue the longest dowel on the front righthand corner of the wood and the other two on each corner of the back. Three thin pieces of wood 5″ long and about as wide as a popsicle stick can form the back side of the crèche, and three 4″ long pieces form the side. Glue the first piece of wood along the back, followed by the side piece which will rest on top of the back piece. Add the next back piece, a side piece, etc., until there are three in back and three on the side. The roof can then be glued on top. It should be 5¾″ long, 4½ ″ wide on one side, and taper down to 1″ wide on the other. Again use very thin wood.

Inside the crèche a round clothespin cut off to be 2½″ tall can represent Joseph, 2″ tall for Mary, and a 1½″ piece for the baby. The leftover clothespin pieces can form the bed: 1¼″ piece for the width and 1¾″ piece for the length. Bits of florist's moss put around inside and on the roof can serve as straw, and a plastic dove on the roof adds an extra touch.

Sunday school classes may enjoy Christmas with an overnighter. The schedule could include caroling in the neighborhood, enjoying a hot snack, telling the Christmas story around a fireplace late at night, and worship in the sanctuary around the altar just before bed, with only the altar lights glowing. Here you might explore with children how they would feel if the Christ child were to be born this year in your town.

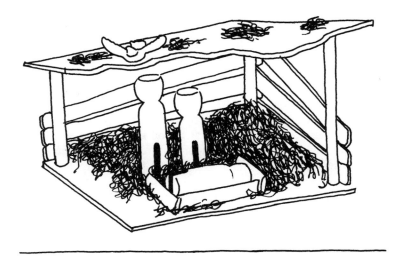

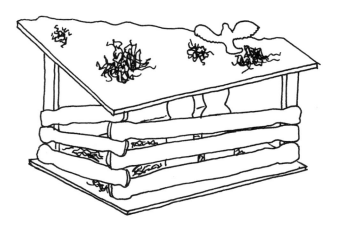

As part of the evening's activities, you might select one foreign country and have a celebration time such as they would have. Christmas legends are also fun to tell, or children might put together a play and videotape it to share with the congregation or with a younger children's class. In this longer time period, a film or videotape could be shown. Banners or other decorations might be created for the classrooms. There are so many ways overnighters can be creative experiences, and they do serve as an evangelism outreach when you allow children to bring outside friends.

One fun way to prepare the classroom is to create a floor-to-ceiling, almost lifesize, nativity MURAL on the wall. Begin by painting long sections of rolled butcher paper, brown or green to represent the ground, and dark blue pieces for sky. The stable can be made with three large pieces of butcher paper painted gray or light brown, representing walls and ceiling. Mary and Joseph can be drawn by having a child lie sideways on top of a large piece of buther paper in a kneeling position and tracing around him/her. Clothing, resembling a robe and head piece, and the facial features need to be drawn. The clothing then should be painted. Jesus can be made by tracing around a doll that has been wrapped in a blanket.

To make sheep, draw an outline on a piece of cardboard and cover the sheep with wool or with cotton balls. A donkey and camels can be made the same way and covered with pieces of gray or brown yarn or paper. Children can cut out stars from yellow construction paper, including one large star. Hang them on yarn from the ceiling. Other figures such as shepherds and wise men, can be added, as the class has time to do so.

One last idea might be to create an outdoor, living NATIVITY SCENE for a Sunday morning or for evenings just before Christmas. Real animals can be used for such scenes in many parts of the country. Churches which provide this kind of setting often become the focal point of a community's Christmas celebration. Many cities no longer allow religious scenes on government land, thus these are lost unless churches do the live scenes.

Advent Wreath and Worship Ceremony

In much of the world, winter is dark and cold. The only greenery available is evergreens which give promise that winter will end and that light and growth will return to earth. Candles symbolize to us that Jesus is the light of the world: he is the inspiration for our lives.

To make an Advent WREATH you need a round piece of styrofoam and five candles (3 purple, 1 pink, and 1 white). The white one is for Christmas and needs to be in the center, the others around the circle. Evergreens, real or artificial, may be added, along with a bright ribbon to fasten along the sides of the styrofoam.

Display the wreath in an important part of the house where family members can gather around it for worship (coffee table, buffet, or dining room table).

Every family should have a manger scene. An inexpensive, unbreakable one is best for children. This allows children to play with it and move the figures around freely. The complete CRÈCHE may be set out on the first Sunday of Advent, or the empty stable could be displayed with animals only. Shepherds can be placed a short distance away to show them grazing their sheep on nearby hills. On the second Sunday of Advent, Mary, Joseph, and the donkey can be placed in another part of the room to show they are traveling. Each week, move Mary and Joseph closer to the stable. On Christmas Eve place them inside, unwrap the baby Jesus, and put him with them. The shepherds can now be placed next to the manger.

The wise men and camels need to be placed in a separate part of the house to show that they had a long journey to make. Each week a family member can move them closer, until Epiphany, twelve days after Christmas, when they can arrive to view the infant Jesus.

First Sunday in Advent

Items needed: Empty crèche, stable animals, Advent wreath, Bible

Adult #1: Today is the first Sunday of Advent—that means we are waiting for the coming of Jesus in our lives. Our stable is empty because it will be four weeks before he will arrive.

Adult #2 There was a man named Isaiah in the Bible who talked about a special child who was to be born for all the people.

Child: (Read Isaiah 9:6-7.)

Adult: Jesus came to show us how to live.

Child:	He is called the "Light of the World."
	(Light the first Candle.)
Child:	Jesus teaches us to love one another.
Adult:	Let us pray: O, God, be a part of our lives, Let the teachings of Jesus rule in our homes. Show us through his love how we can love each other. Amen.
	(Child should put the animals into the stable.)
Closing:	Play Christmas carols at the conclusion of the service.

Second Sunday in Advent

Items needed:	Mary, Joseph, and donkey figures wrapped in paper, Bible, Advent wreath
Adult #1:	Jesus was born into a family. Mary and Joseph had to travel from Nazareth to Bethlehem just before Jesus' birth. They were poor and had only a donkey on which to ride.
Adult #2:	Please unwrap Mary and Joseph and the donkey. *(Give to child.)*
Child:	*(Set figures down.)* Here are the parents of Jesus. God knew he needed a father and mother to love him.
Parent:	(Read Luke 2:1-7.)
Child:	The first candle reminds us that Jesus is the light of the world. The second candle reminds us of the love of Jesus' family and of our love for each other. *(Light two Advent candles.)* A carol to be said or sung: "O Little Town of Bethlehem"
Prayer:	May the love of Jesus and his family be with our family tonight and throughout this coming week. Amen. *(Take Mary and Joseph and donkey to part of house to begin their journey from Nazareth.)*

Third Sunday in Advent

Items needed:	Shepherds and sheep wrapped in paper, Bible, and Advent wreath.

Adult:	Imagine what it is like to be a shepherd outside at night with your sheep, watching the stars and thinking about God.
Child:	*(Unwrap shepherds and sheep.)* A shepherd loves and cares for his sheep and Jesus is like a shepherd who loves us.
Adult:	Listen to the story of the shepherds. (Read Luke 2:8-16.)
Child:	The first Advent candle reminds us that Jesus is the light of the world. The second candle tells us of the love of his family. The third candle is for the shepherds who came to visit the baby Jesus. *(Light three Advent candles.)* Sing or say: "While Shepherds Watched Their Flocks by Night"
Prayer:	*(all together)* O God, open our eyes. Help us to see that Jesus came for all people—for lowly shepherds and also for each one of us. Help us to live as Jesus taught us. Amen." *(Place the shepherds and sheep near the manger.)*

Fourth Sunday in Advent

Items needed:	Wise men and camels, wrapped, Bible and Advent wreath.
Adult:	This is Christmas Sunday. It is only a short time until Jesus' birthday. Let's share together a special way in which we have given love to others this Advent season. *(All share.)*
Adult:	Today we unwrap the wise men and camels and place them across the room. They gave their love and gifts to Jesus and traveled from far away to visit him. They are a symbol that Jesus came to help the rich and wise as well as the poor and humble. *Read Matthew 2:1-12.*
Read or sing:	"We Three Kings of Orient Are."
Adult:	Each of the candles reminds us of something, the

first that Jesus is the light of the world. The second candle tells us about Mary and Joseph and their love.

Child: The third candle is for the shepherds who visited Jesus, and the fourth candle is for the wise men who are traveling to bring him gifts.

Prayer: God help us to give to others as the wise men gave to Jesus . . . and show us new ways to share love this special season. In Jesus' name we pray. Amen.

(Place the wise men far off in another room or across the room.)

Christmas Day, December 25

Items needed: Wrapped figures of Jesus, Bible, Advent wreath, Mary and Joseph should be in manger already.

Adult: At last it is Christmas, the time when Jesus was born. Let us read the Christmas story from the Bible.

Adult: (Read Luke 2:1-20.)
Child unwraps the baby Jesus.

Child says (or all sing): "Away in a Manger."

Light all the candles.

Adult: This last candle we light because Christmas is here and Jesus is the most special Christmas gift in the world.

Child: It is Jesus' birthday.

Adult: It's a day to show love.

Child: It's a day to pray for peace on earth.

Adult: It's a day to worship God and thank God for all our blessings.

Prayer: Thank you, God, for all we have and all we share. And thank you most of all for the gift of your Son. Help us to share our love and bring us peace always. Amen.

(Put Jesus into the manger and bring the shepherds to see the baby Jesus. Today the three wise men might be

*moved into the same room as the crèche but not close to
it, to represent the travels of these men.)*

Advent Calendar

This may be made on construction paper, red or green; 9" x 12" size works best.

Begin your calendar with the first Sunday of Advent rather than December since this is more correct. On some years the calendar will begin with the last Sunday in November.

By holding the paper the long way, draw eight vertical lines 1½" apart, leaving a small margin on all four edges. This will make enough spaces for each day of the week. Horizontal lines that are 2" apart, again leaving a space top and bottom, will divide the calendar into 4 weeks. Lines need to be drawn on both pieces of paper, with the date and pictures or stickers on the cover page and typed or printed special things to do on the second page. The two pages then need to be glued together around the edges. Instructions on the back can invite children to cut out one day at a time and follow the instructions on the inside. An adult can help get the first cut started in the thick paper.

Ideas for Advent calendar:

1. Make a family Advent wreath and light the first Advent candle.
2. With your family, select a special guest to come to dinner one night this month.
3. Share together the meaning of Advent as the time for Jesus' birth.
4. Set up the crèche and have family worship time. Read Luke 11:1-4.
5. Write a family letter to a friend far away.
6. Take flowers or cookies to a neighbor.
7. Shop for a gift for a needy person.
8. Bring canned foods to church for the food pantry and light the second Advent candle.
9. Call someone far away to say, "I love you."
10. Listen to Christmas music during dinner.
11. Read Luke 2:1-20 in family worship.
12. Plan together a way to help a friend or neighbor.

13. Rent a Christmas video and enjoy it as a family.
14. Read a Christmas legend together.
15. Greet someone whom you don't know at church. Light the third Advent candle.
16. Have a meatless dinner and give an offering to world hunger.
17. Take a short drive and enjoy Christmas lights.
18. Read Luke 2:27-35 in family worship.
19. Phone another church friend to say "Merry Christmas."
20. Write a special note of thanks to your Sunday school teacher, pastor, or other church staff person.
21. Bake some cookies and share them.
22. Make an ornament for the Christmas tree. Light the fourth Advent candle.
23. Enjoy a family evening: wrap gifts and play games; no television.
24. Discuss together the lessons Jesus taught.
25. Read Matthew 2:1-12.
26. Choose a family prayer time and pray for peace on earth.
27. Work as a family cleaning the house for Christmas.
28. It's Christmas Eve—light the fifth Advent candle and attend worship as a family.

CELEBRATING CHRISTMAS IN FAMILY SETTINGS

Establishing family customs around Christmas can give this holiday real depth and meaning beyond what the retail world promotes. Use this as a time to share with children your faith and commitment to Jesus as Lord and Savior. The ritual of the Advent wreath ceremony and regular worship attendance in church can let the child know Christmas is indeed a time to celebrate the birth of the Christ child in our lives.

Plan to do many things together as a family; DECORATE the house and tree, send cards, bake cookies, work on a Christmas guest list, and wrap packages together. Children enjoy stories of the past, so share yours of Christmas when you were a child. Play Christmas music and read a book of legends from the library or purchased from a bookstore. Visit special religious displays in your town, such as a community nativity scene, and attend special religious plays and musicals at church. Even young children can gain an appreciation of the meaning of Christmas this way.

Instead of a fancy decorated TREE, create an old-fashioned one decorated with pine cones, candies, cookies, cranberry, and popcorn strings, or make a tree of homemade decorations in which all family members can share.

FLAGS on the tree are a tradition in Scandinavian countries. These are easy to make, requiring only paper, string, marking pen, and scissors. Paper should be cut double the size of the finished product and folded in half, with the fold being at the top of the flag. Children can choose the flags of as many different countries as they desire, and color the designs on both sides of the paper. String will be strung through the top of the fold. Then place the flags on the tree vertically from top to bottom, which is typical of Scandinavian flags.

Some families make CHRISMONS (ornaments made from paper, styrofoam, or wood in the shape of Christian symbols). Usually these are white, but gold glitter or paint may trim each ornament.

Establish a custom of reading the Christmas story before opening gifts and of having a time of prayer for a peaceful world.

Guests can bring so much meaning to a holiday; so whether your family is large or small, invite others in to be a part of this special day.

This might also be a time to celebrate a few Christmas traditions of your own cultural heritage or those of another culture.

Share with children the story of ST. NICHOLAS, a Roman Catholic Bishop, who reportedly distributed gifts to children at this season. A tradition developed of honoring this man on December 6 by distributing gifts, and Dutch seamen are reported to have brought this idea with them to the colonies. The American Santa Claus developed from this tradition.

Celebrate St. Nicholas Day by having children leave their SHOES out to be filled. Small gifts wrapped in disguise packages can be placed in the shoes.

Santa Lucia Day in Sweden is December 13. The eldest daughter, dressed in a white gown with red ribbon waistband and wearing a crown of lights, brings breakfast to the family: lucia buns and coffee.

Swedish Coffee Buns

2	c. scalded milk	1	egg, beaten
3	tbl. shortening	⅓	c. warm water
2	pkge. dry yeast	6	c. flour
1	c. sugar	6	crushed cardamom seeds
1	tsp. salt		

Melt shortening in hot milk, let cool. Dissolve yeast in warm water and add sugar, salt, beaten egg, and seeds. Add flour. Let stand to rise for 2 hours in a warm place. Punch down, form into shapes. Roll pieces of dough into cigar-like shapes and form the shapes into a spiral-like circle. Push a few raisins into the creases of dough on each bun. Brush tops with beaten egg and sprinkle with sugar. Bake at 400° about 15 minutes.

Choose a day to feed the birds. Feasts for the birds are prepared on outdoor trees and in feeding stations. Bird seeds, bags of suet, and peanut butter spread on pine cones will be enjoyed by the wildlife; and it is one way to say to children that we care about the small creatures of God's creation.

Arrange family Christmas CARDS in the shape of a tree or wreath on a door, fireplace, or wall. A wreath of cards can be created by using a wire circle or styrofoam ring and attaching cards to it.

JEWISH HOLIDAYS

PURIM

Purim is a holiday to celebrate the Jews' triumph over evil and oppression. The Book of Esther tells an ancient tale of such an event. As the story is told, when King Ahasuerus (Xerxes) was ruler of Persia, he ordered Vashti, his queen, to dance at a party of his friends. When she refused, he had her removed, and later, after a search, chose Esther (secretly a Jew) as his new queen.

Haman, the king's chief officer, plotted against the Jews by asking the king to order everyone to bow down and worship him. When they refused (since such homage could be given only to God), Haman plotted their execution. Esther rescued her people by pleading mercy from the king. In the end, it was Haman, not the Jews, who was hanged.

No one is certain of the authenticity of this story since there is no record in Persian history of the people or events mentioned in the book. Some scholars believe that a holiday (probably the Babylonian new year celebration in which the gods, Marduk and Istar, cast lots [purim] to determine each other's fates) was a forerunner of Purim. Perhaps the elements of this pagan festival were borrowed and transformed into the story of Esther by Jews returning from their exile as a way of continuing what had become a most popular celebration in a foreign land.

The story of Esther is further complicated because it is the only book of the Bible which never mentions God by the special name Yahweh, although a rewritten version can be found in the Apocryphal books of the Septuagint, the Greek translation of the Hebrew Scriptures.

Nevertheless every year around the first of March, Jews remember this story and the subsequent triumphs over their enemies throughout history, especially the evil of Hitler during World War II. It is a time to remember to be faithful to God no matter who the oppressors are.

In synagogue services the Scroll of Esther is read in its entirety, and whenever the name Haman is spoken, the congregation boos, stamps their feet, and shakes noisemakers similar to ones which are used on New Year's Eve.

Thanksgiving-like feasts are enjoyed, gifts given to special friends and neighbors, and charity shown to the needy. Often people attend costume balls, and children participate in carnivals with games and prizes offered. Many years ago it was a time for house-to-house begging by children, such as trick or treating is today; and people would build large bonfires in order to burn Haman in effigy.

One special food for Purim is *hamanthaschen*, a delicious triangle-shaped tart filled with poppy seeds or fruit. Its shape is supposed to resemble Haman's hat.

Hamantaschen

⅔	c. sugar	1	tsp. vanilla extract
2	eggs		Grated rind of ½ orange
½	c. oil	3	c. flour
	jam	1½	tsp. baking powder

Beat eggs until thick. Add sugar, oil, and flavorings. Stir in enough flour to make a rollable dough. Roll out on floured board. Cut in 2" squares. Place a spoonful of filling (apricot jam or others) in center of square. Fold dough over to form a triangle. Brush tops with a little beaten egg. Bake at 350° approximately 30 minutes.

PURIM IN SUNDAY SCHOOL SETTINGS

As class begins, children may make noisemakers or rattles called *greggars*. Juice or other metal cans filled with stones or buttons, then covered with paper on all sides is one way to do this. Paper plates can also be stapled together and filled with the same items.

Girls may make Queen Esther crowns of tagboard, attaching sequins and old jewelry to give it a rich appearance, while boys might make Haman's hat. According to tradition this is to be three-cornered, triangular shaped. It may also be made of tagboard, with each side approximately 8" long and 4" wide. By stapling all the ends together children will form the hat. Boys may paint them in various colors.

When projects have been completed, share the story of Queen Esther. (It will be more interesting if it is memorized rather than read from a book.) Information about Purim should also be given. The class may enjoy a short role play of the story or enjoy pretending to be in a synagogue worship service. The one who is the "rabbi" should read parts from the Book of Esther while participants boo Haman and rattle the *greggars* whenever his name is mentioned. They might also print Haman's name with chalk on the soles of their shoes and "stamp out Haman" as the reading progresses.

It is a Jewish custom to give charitable gifts to needy families during Purim; so an offering may be taken for this purpose, or children may be asked to bring canned foods to class on "Purim" day.

As an alternate activity, plan a visit to a synagogue service or inquire about participating in a children's Purim carnival. A time to meet with a rabbi and learn more about Jewish traditions should also be a part of any visit. Of course, a class might plan their own Purim carnival and invite other Sunday school classes to participate. Children who are used to school carnivals will have many ideas for games and activities to share. *Hamantaschen* may be eaten or sold as a carnival treat.

This is probably the favorite of all Jewish celebrations, and it certainly combines the most elaborate home rituals of any Jewish holidays. It is a three-fold celebration as indicated by its various names.

The festival of Spring *(Hag Ha-Aviv)* refers to a spring barley festival of ancient Egypt where the people harvested their first barley crops and baked them into unleavened cakes, offering thanks to the deity for a good harvest. This marked the beginning of a forty-nine day celebration which ended on Shavuot, the fiftieth day.

Later this was altered. Exodus 12:39 tells the story of the slaves who baked unleavened cakes before fleeing Egypt since there was no time to allow the bread to rise. In Exodus 23:15 they are charged with keeping the Feast of Unleavened Bread for seven days to remember their ancestors' sojourn from slavery to freedom in a new land. Thus its second name is *Hag Ha-Matzot* or Festival of Unleavened Bread.

It was also the practice of some primitive cultures to sacrifice a lamb each spring in order to please the gods and to protect the rest of the flock from harm. In Exodus 12:11 this ritual became the smearing of lamb's blood on the doorposts of the slaves' homes in order for God to know them and "pass over" them, inflicting harm only on the firstborn of the Egyptian households. Thus the holiday received its more popular name of *Seder* (Sā'der) or Passover.

This festival of spring, usually, falling in April, is celebrated by most Jews for seven days, though Conservative and Orthodox Jews add an additional day. Ancient calendars were not very dependable, so people were notified of this holiday by mountaintop bonfires. However, to guard against anyone being late for Passover, an extra day was added.

Hametz is a Hebrew word which means leaven. Foods with leavening are strictly forbidden during Passover. The original prohibition carried a powerful ritual taboo. Indeed the Torah dictates (in Exodus) a severe punishment of excommunication for even owning *hametz* during Passover. This led to three curious customs: first a thorough cleaning of one's house to remove all leaven, then hiding a few crumbs of bread, followed by a search conducted by candle, spoon, and feather to find the last remnants of leaven and scoop it up into the spoon using the feather. Finally, there was the custom of selling all leavened products to non-Jewish neighbors, and repurchasing it at the conclusion of the holiday.

Matzoth is the traditional unleavened bread of this season and is known by Jews and non-Jews. It certainly existed longer than the holiday celebration or even the Exodus. Sarah is said to have served it to the three strangers who visited her and Abraham. Perhaps it was used as food for unexpected guests because it could be hastily prepared. (See Genesis 18:6.) For Passover, a special matzoth is reserved, one that has been watched during the growing and harvesting process to make certain there is no extra moisture which would begin the leavening process.

The traditional way to celebrate this holiday is with a Seder meal followed by a big dinner.

The Seder table is prepared with place settings for every guest and an extra one for Elijah the absent guest; wine glasses for every place, and the Seder plate on which is placed:

1. flat matzoth, a reminder that there was no time to allow the bread to rise when the slaves fled from Egypt;
2. hardboiled egg, symbolizing fertility, goodness, and many years of prosperity;
3. lamb bone, a remembrance of the lamb sacrifice of our ancestors in the smearing of lamb's blood on the doorposts;
4. bitter herbs, horseradish to remember the bitterness of slavery;
5. *karpas,* sprig of parsley, a symbol of spring, the season of hope;
6. *charoset,* apples, nuts, honey, and cinnamon mixed together to represent the mortar used to make bricks when our ancestors were slaves.

A dish of saltwater, symbolic of tears shed by the enslaved people, is placed on the table. Copies of the Seder ceremony may be purchased from B'nai B'rith, 315 Lexington Av., New York, N. Y. 10016, and often may be obtained from Jewish synagogues as well. Some grocery stores in urban areas carry copies upon request. The Seder meal is described in Exodus 12:3-11 and Deuteronomy 6:20-21 but actually became popular as a home celebration after the temple was destroyed.

Jesus celebrated the Passover according to several gospel passages (John 2:12-14, 23 and John 6:3-6). Since this was also part of the last supper of Jesus and his disciples, this holiday has greater significance to Christians than other Jewish special days; but it has been modified to the receiving of bread and wine or grape juice. We should take note that Jesus was described as the last paschal lamb, thereby eliminating all future lamb sacrifices for sin.

PASSOVER WITH CHILDREN IN SUNDAY SCHOOL

Open Bibles to the story of the Passover in Exodus 12 and also Jesus' Last Supper, Mark 14:12-26. Read and discuss these two stories. It is also important to retell the story of Moses and the exodus.

Children might like to make a class frieze (series of pictures which depict the exodus story), or a MURAL, scene of the Hebrew people traveling through the desert in search of the promised land. On a long sheet of paper paint the background, brown earth, rocks, patches of green, cacti, and a few palm trees. Then draw the people, animals, and tents and glue them onto the mural as soon as it is dry.

Make a SEDER PLATE with crayon pictures of the parsley, egg charoset, lamb bone, matzoth, and horseradish. Children might print out the name and meaning of each item on the back of the plate.

Celebrate a simplified Seder meal together using the enclosed ritual, or a short communion service with matzoth and grape juice; and share the new meaning which Passover (or Last Supper) has for Christians.

Items needed: paper plate, fork, napkin, and cup at each child's place, Seder plate in center of table with items as listed above, and also a dish of salty water in front of the "father" and a larger plate with three or more pieces of matzoth. Each child should also have his/her cup filled with grape juice. Someone should be chosen to be the father at the Seder meal, and one child to ask the questions. At this time the celebration of the Seder begins.

Seder Ritual

Father: "Blessed are you, O Lord, our God, King of the Universe who gives us life and who has let us exist until now." *(He holds up the cup and all children sip the grape juice.)*

Father: *(Holds up the parsley, dips it into salty water, and says):* "Blessed are you, O Lord our God, creator of the earth." *(Each child should taste the parsley.)*

Then Father takes the middle piece of matzoth, breaks it in half and hides half of it under his plate (or some place close by). He passes out the rest of the matzoth to everyone. Then he holds up his piece of matzoth and everyone says: "This is the flat bread which our ancestors ate in the wilderness. There was no time for the bread to rise. Whoever wishes to, let him or her come and celebrate Passover with us."

Child: "Why is this night different from all other nights? On all other nights we eat either bread or matzoth but tonight we eat only matzoth. On all other nights we eat vegetables, but tonight we eat only bitter herbs."

Father: "Our ancestors once were slaves in Egypt. It is right for us to remember their enslavement."

At this point allow children to tell what they remember of the Exodus story. When all have had a turn to speak, continue the ritual.

Father holds up the horseradish, "Why do we eat the bitter herb? Because our ancestors' lives were bitter at the hands of the Egyptians." Allow children to spread a little horseradish on pieces of matzoth and eat it. Then everyone raises a cup.

Everyone: "We must thank and praise God who has brought us out of slavery to freedom. Hallelujah!" *(All may drink some of their grape juice.)*

Father holds up the shankbone and says, "This lamb bone, symbol of the Passover sacrifice, reminds us that God blessed us by passing over the houses of our ancestors in Egypt, sparing us." He holds up the *haroset*. "This *haroset* reminds us that they were forced to make bricks for their captors. *Haroset* resembles the mortar with which they sealed the bricks." Allow children to eat *haroset* with matzoth. At this time children may finish their crackers and then report to the Father where the hidden piece of matzoth is. (This is called the *afekomen*.) When found it should be broken and shared with all. Then the ritual continues:

Father: "Let us say grace."
Everyone: "May God's name be praised forever."
Father: "Praise and thanks to God, ruler of the universe who gives us all food. Remember us this day in kindness."
Everyone: "Give us your blessing today. Amen."
Father: "Next year may we be in Jerusalem."

Seder Meal

1. Matzo
2. Hard-boiled egg
3. Lamb bone
4. Horseradish
5. Sprig of parsley
6. Haroset (mixture of apples, nuts, honey, and cinnamon)

This holiday began as an ancient agricultural festival celebrating the barley harvest. Israelite farmers donated a portion of their food to God in recognition of the One who protects the crops.

Counting of Omer was originally part of this forty-nine day period. (Omer is a measurement used in weighing barley.) In this practice Jews were almost in agreement with the Canaanite (nature) religion which stated that God and humankind were in partnership, and harvest offerings were a recognition of this fact. Grain offerings were left in the temple each day. See Leviticus 23:17.

Shavuoth is a Hebrew word meaning weeks. This holiday has also been called the Festival of the Harvest *(Hag Hokatzer)*, day of the First Fruits (Deuteronomy 16:9-12), and Pentecost. It falls fifty days after Passover and marks the conclusion of this season. It is not a holiday mandated in the Old Testament, as are other Jewish days, and for this reason was left in some dispute. Among Orthodox Jews, it was a two-day celebration but today is celebrated only for one day by Reform Jews.

Forty-nine days, according to legend, are the number of days it took the freed slaves to travel from Egypt to the foot of Mt. Sinai. Thus the Torah or giving of the ten commandments (Exodus 19 and 20) has come to be associated with Shavuoth.

The important laws of Judaism are always read in the synagogue at this time, and the scroll of Ruth is read also because she gleaned the fields (legend says at this time of year). She's also the great-grand-mother of David. Her sense of responsibility to Naomi and conversion to Judaism are considered important. Legend connects David's birth and death to the season of Shavuoth.

In Israel, it is a day for pilgrimages to David's tomb and the lighting of 150 candles (one for each Psalm). Other customs of the day include eating dairy foods, especially cheesecake and cheese blintzes, symbolizing the "sweetness of the Torah" and the land of milk and honey where the freed people would finally settle. Another explanation of this custom is that people returning to their tents after receiving the Ten Commandments were so weary and hungry they couldn't wait to cook and so ate the handiest foods available, which were cheese and milk.

Christian Whitsun or Pentecost has similarities to this Jewish holiday. When the disciples and friends of Jesus gathered on the day of Pentecost (see Acts 2) and received the Holy Spirit, the day became known as the birthday of the Christian church. In a similar way, on Shavuoth Jews celebrate receiving the Ten Commandments, the Torah, and the birth of the Jewish faith.

Cheese Blintzes

Pancake:

3	eggs	1¼	c. flour
1¼	c. sugar	2	tbl. shortening
pinch of salt			

Mix all ingredients thoroughly, beating until smooth. Melt shortening in a skillet and pour a small amount of batter into it. Spread it out to fill the pan (easily done by lifting and tilting the pan). Pancake should be thin. Turn pancake over as soon as it is done on one side. (The edges will no longer stick to the sides of the pan.) Remove from pan onto a plate when done. Make all pancakes first and then add the filling.

Filling:

1	(8 oz.) package cream cheese or cottage cheese	1	egg yolk
		1	tsp. vanilla
1	lb. farmer cheese	3	tsp. sugar

Blend cheeses in a food processor. Combine rest of ingredients. Mix until smooth but not blended. Put filling inside each pancake and roll like a scroll. Scroll shape is said to resemble the Ten Commandments and be a reminder of the giving of the law. Pancakes may be kept warm in a 200° oven or heated quickly in a microwave before serving.

SHAVUOTH IN SUNDAY SCHOOL

Children who arrive early might arrange flowers and fresh fruits on the worship table and open the Bible to Deuteronomy 16:16-17 (background information for this holiday). Those who will take part in the closing worship should also be selected.

Explain to the class the STORY of SHAVUOTH and the two separate traditions connected to it. Divide the children into two groups. One group studies the story of Ruth and works on a short skit to present to the rest of the class. The other group studies the story of Moses and the presentation of the Ten Commandments to his followers in the desert. They can write the commandments out on a large scroll which may be decorated with vines and flowers along the sides. A short role play of the story of Moses is another idea for this group.

Gather everyone together for the last twenty minutes of class time and allow each to share what he/she has learned. The teacher will add the story of Pentecost and the experiences of Jesus' followers.

Worship

First child:	(Read Deuteronomy 16:16-17.)
Second child:	"At *Shavuoth* we remember the story of Ruth who left her homeland to travel with Naomi to a new land."
Third child:	(Read Ruth 1: 16-17.)
Fourth child:	"This day is also called 'law day' by the Jews and is the time when they received the Ten Commandments." *(Read them from the class scroll.)*

Close with prayer, thanking God for giving us rules by which to live and holidays so we will remember them. If there is time, enjoy a treat of crackers, cheese, and milk.

An alternate suggestion for this study might be to divide the room into Moab and Bethlehem. String a wire high across the room and hang sheets or blankets from the wire. Additionally, if your room has two doors, it would be good to have one door in each "country."

In Moab create a TENT with canvass or blankets. Inside show a filmstrip about Ruth, or have a teacher in costume pretend to be Ruth and tell her story. Across from the tent should be a table and clay for molding clay statue gods, such as the people of Moab worshiped.

Explain to the children the kinds of gods worshiped here and the new faith which Ruth was to embrace. When the children have finished with these activities, help them summarize briefly what they have learned. Make up a chant by reciting Ruth 1:16b and clapping in rhythm as you do so. Rehearse it a few times, then do it all together repeatedly as you march out the door into the hall and back into the other part of the room where Bethlehem is.

In this new room, gather the class together, share the rest of the story of Ruth, and tell them of its relationship to *Shavuoth* and why it is called "law day." Children may then move into one of three new learning centers.

1. Role play center to dramatize the story of Ruth.

2. Ten Commandment table, a study of the "law."
3. Pentecost table. Here children will learn about the Christian holiday celebrated at almost the same time as *Shavuoth*.

For the last part of class have each group share what they have learned. Cheese and milk may be served, with an explanation about the connection between these two foods and this holiday.

Rosh Hashanah First Day of Tishri

This holiday marks the beginning of Jewish high holy days and may fall either in September or October, depending upon the calendar. It is traditionally called the celebration of the New Year but actually falls in the seventh month (Tishri). It is more the agricultural new year than the actual date, as Nisan is the first month of the Jewish calendar. This day, along with Yom Kippur ten days later, forms the two holiest days of Judaism. The date was believed to have been chosen because an ancient Babylonian "Day of Judgment," associated with the god Marduk, was connected to this time of year. Jews in exile there most likely borrowed elements of this day in shaping Rosh Hashanah.

It is a time of remembrance, repentance, judgment, repayment of debts, and blowing of the *shofar*. A belief developed that God judged every Jew on this day and sealed the names of the righteous in a book. Others had a ten-day period in which to ask God's forgiveness and also ask forgiveness from friends or family for any wrongs done to them before having their fate sealed for a good or bad new year. It is a deeply religious season when sincere Jews examine their lives and try to make restitution for their sins.

The observance begins with the reading of the *Selechot* (meaning forgiveness) on the Saturday before Rosh Hashanah. Then on the eve of the holiday, they recite the words for the festival candle and Kiddush over a round *hallah* (loaf of bread) just before dinner. It is eaten along with honey cake (recipe included) and apples sweetened with honey. These foods symbolize hope that the fates will be sealed for a sweet new year. The round *hallah* resembles a crown and symbolizes the kingship of God.

No one knows why apples are chosen instead of other fruits, but mystical powers for promoting good health were once ascribed to this fruit (hence, "an apple a day keeps the doctor away"). In addition, though the fruit of the garden of Eden is never mentioned, the apple has always been a symbol associated with this story.

The Rosh Hashanah greeting *"Leshanah tovah tiktavi"* (may you be inscribed for a good new year) generally came to be recited during the Middle Ages. Today, greeting cards with these words will be exchanged.

As worship services begin in the evening, someone blows the

shofar, a ram's horn symbolic of the ram which appeared to Abraham as he was about to sacrifice Isaac to God in Genesis 22:13. Read Numbers 29:1-11 for a description of this day.

Honey Cake *(Lekah)*

2 c. flour	2 eggs
2 tsp. cinnamon	½ tsp. baking soda, dissolved
¾ c. sugar	in ½ c. orange juice
2 tsp. ginger	½ c. chopped walnuts
¾ c. honey	grated orange rind
½ c. cooking oil	

Mix sugar, flour, and spices. Add honey, oil, and eggs. Beat until smooth. Add orange juice and baking soda. Fold in nuts and grated orange rind, if desired. Bake in 10"x 8" pan at 350° until done.

YOM KIPPUR

This day means "Day of Atonement" and is considered the holiest period of the Jewish calendar. Most Jews will attend synagogue even if they have failed to do so at any other time of year. The observance dates from early in Hebrew history and is recorded in the Torah (first five books of the Bible), in several places, including Leviticus 16:29-34 and 23:26-32. Legend connects the story of receiving the Ten Commandments with this date as well. Moses came down only to discover his people worshiping a golden calf. In anger Moses broke the tablets and had to reascend Mt. Sinai for replacements. When he returned ten days later (said to be the tenth day of Tishri) with the new tablets, he found the people fasting and repentant. Thus they received God's forgiveness (Exodus 32:19-34).

In ancient times, the day was observed by presenting two goats before the altar of the temple (Leviticus 16:7-22). One was sacrificed as a sin offering; the other had the sins of the people heaped upon it by a priest and was driven into the wilderness, hence the origin of the term, *scapegoat.*

Once the temple was destroyed, Yom Kippur became a day of complete rest from all work. Prayer, worship, fasting for twenty-four hours, and giving of charitable gifts were all observed. At this time a new ritual appeared, that of holding a chicken by the neck over one's head and whirling it around three times in order to absolve one's sin. The animal was then slaughtered and the meat given to the poor.

Today fasting is considered important and is observed by all healthy adult Jews and children over the age of twelve or thirteen. They believe it is possible to spend more time in prayer by not eating. Pregnant women and those who are ill or being persecuted (as in World War II) are not expected to fast.

Attendance in worship is required in order to "get right with God," although wrongs to people have to be corrected by requesting forgiveness from those wronged. The Book of Jonah is read in the service as proof of God's mercy to a repentant people.

White is the symbolic color of the day. Altar cloths and garments of the rabbi reflect this. It is taken from scripture in Isaiah 1:18 which says, "Though your sins be as scarlet they shall become white as snow." A service for the dead is said, and the day concludes with the final blowing of the *shofar.*

People then go home and break the fast with an elaborate meal. They often eat a special *hallah* bread which is braided or shaped like a bird, symbolizing the hope of Jews to ascend spiritually to the level of angels. Their greeting, *gemar Hatimah tovah,* means "May you be sealed for good."

Hallah

2	pkge. dry yeast	1	tsp. salt
1	c. plus 2 tbl. warm water	5	c. all-purpose flour
⅔	c. sugar		Poppy seeds to sprinkle on top
½	c. vegetable oil		

Dissolve the yeast in warm water, add oil, sugar, and salt; mix well. Gradually add flour. Knead dough for ten minutes, place in a greased bowl, cover with a cloth and place in a warm place to rise—for about two hours. When ready, divide the bread into two loaves, and place on two oiled baking sheets. Cover and allow to rise again for one hour. Brush with melted butter and sprinkle poppy seeds on top. Bake at 375° for 30-35 minutes or until brown.

ROSH HASHANAH AND YOM KIPPUR WITH CHILDREN

Since these two holidays constitute the high holy days, it is appropriate to study them together.

Begin by making *yarmulkes* (HATS, pattern on following page). These are worn by conservative male Jews when they attend synagogue and by Orthodox Jews daily. *Shofars* (RAM'S HORNS) can be made with two pieces of paper cut like a horn and stapled together; stuff shredded or thin crumpled paper inside to make the horns three-dimensional.

When these activities are completed, describe the significance of these two days and read together the verses in the Bible which tell about them: Numbers 29:1-11 and Leviticus 16:29-34.

Since this is a season of repentance and forgiveness, tell the story of the prodigal son to show the extent of God's forgiveness when we go astray, and discuss times when we all need forgiveness. Let each child write his or her own PRAYER for forgiveness. New Year's resolutions may also be written, sealed in an envelope, and kept by children until they receive a postcard or letter from the teacher (in two or three months) telling them to open the resolutions and examine how well they have kept them.

Honey cake may be served as a SNACK. Close with one or more of the prayers written by the children.

Pattern for Yarmulke

Cut 6 pieces. They may be blue, black, or white. Join straight edges together by taping to make a cap.

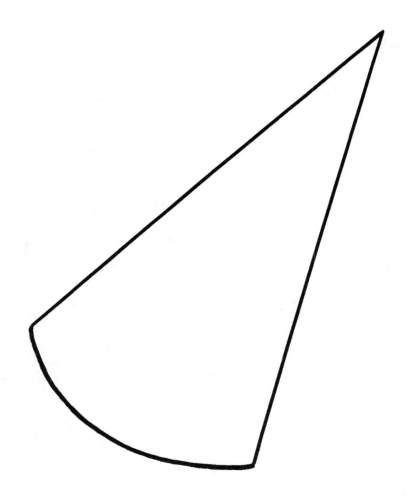

SUCCOTH

This holiday arrives five days after Yom Kippur and is also called "Feast of the Tabernacles," "Feast of the Lord," or "Feast of Ingathering." See Leviticus 23:33-44. The scripture refers to this celebration as an agricultural festival which was originally held after crops were gathered, the date changing each year to coincide with harvest time. It is observed for seven days by most Jews today and reflects the forty-year wilderness experience of Moses and his followers in the desert.

After the destruction of the Temple in A.D. 70, succoth (or sukkoth) became a celebration of home and synagogue. *Sukah* is a word which means booth or shelter, and such temporary huts were built in synagogue and home as a reminder that Moses and his followers lived in similar structures during their long wanderings in the wilderness. Actually, temporary shelters were found often in fields and were used by harvesters for resting and protection from the sun.

The *sukah* is to be a three-sided structure, the fourth side being open. Size is unimportant, but it must hold at least one person. The roof is to be temporary, covered with leaves and tree branches, but allowing light to enter so stars may shine through at night. The walls and sides are laden with branches and hanging fruits. In Bible times, only men and boys would sleep in them; but entire families often ate their meals inside.

This is a happy celebration of Thanksgiving after the solemn high holy days. Today few Jews build booths and prefer leaving this to the synagogue where special blessings are recited throughout the seven-day period. A symbolic booth is built, and the altar is laden with a colorful display of harvested crops.

Waving a palm branch, myrtle branch, and citron *(Etrog)* held in a three-sectioned holder called a *lulav* symbolizes that God is everywhere. Leviticus 23:40 describes this curious ceremony which dates back to pre-Jewish traditions. In addition the willow symbolized the mouth (uttering prayer); citron, the heart (for wisdom and understanding); *lulav,* the spine (for upright behavior); and myrtle, the eyes (of learning and knowledge).

Orthodox Jews consider the first two days to be solemn holidays and abstain from work. Though the eighth day is extra, it is often a day for prayers for rain and special memorial services for the dead.

CELEBRATING SUCCOTH WITH CHILDREN

Here is an opportunity to teach children about a Thanksgiving celebration that far predates the pilgrims' holiday. Help them discover the many things for which they can be thankful.

As children arrive, have them build a large BOOTH (or an individual booth can be made with shoeboxes, leafy branches, and paper fruit). A three-sided wooden frame is needed. Use twine to tie them together, then add leafy branches and fresh fruits and vegetables. As you work, share with the children information about the history of the booth. When the booth is finished, read from the Bible (Leviticus 23:39-43).

John 7:1-13 records that Jesus and his disciples celebrated this holiday. Ask children how Jesus and the disciples could do this since they traveled so much, staying with friends and sometimes sleeping outdoors. Compare the Hebrew Thanksgiving with the way we celebrate ours today.

A thanksgiving PLAY is included here; your class might like to rehearse it to present to another class or perhaps make a videotape to show parents.

Thanksgiving Play

Narrator: This is TV station ____ ____ ____ of the ____ ____ Church. It's time to look back into history once more . . . into the lives of Old Testament families. Today we will be learning something about the Hebrew people's harvest festival or thanksgiving time. The family is building a booth made of leafy branches in the yard. . . . Let's listen to them.

Mary: Why are we building this booth?

Father: Why? Well, to celebrate the harvest time and to remember that long ago our ancestors lived in booths as they travelled across the desert.

David: It is written in the Torah in the laws (read Leviticus 23:39-42).

Jon: And we get to sleep in the booth for a whole week!

Esther: Do I get to sleep in it, too?

Jon: No, you're a girl. Only the men and boys can sleep in it.

Esther: But I want to sleep in it, too! Can't I, Father?

Father: No, but we all will live in the booth during the day.

Mother: Yes, Esther and Mary, you can help me prepare food and we'll eat all of our meals in the booth for seven whole days!

Mary: And will we be thanking God for the good harvest?

Mother: Yes, dear. That is the reason for this booth.

Father: Come. Let us finish building this booth so that we can begin to live inside!

Narrator: Now it is dinner time in the booth. . . . Let's listen to Father as he speaks. . . .

Father: As you know, there are two reasons we celebrate Succoth . . . One is to thank God for the harvest and the other is to remember Moses and the trip our ancestors took through the wilderness. They lived in booths like this one as they traveled.

Mother: May our home be blessed, O God, by the light of love and good will bringing blessing to us and to all of Israel. *(She lights a candle.)*

Whole Family: We praise thee, O God, for life and harvest.

Father: These fruits are a symbol of joy. Let us thank God who is king of the universe.

Narrator: And so you see how the Hebrew people long ago celebrated thanksgiving. Today they still celebrate this holiday by special prayers and attending services in the synagogue. Some Jews still build the booth at home to remember Moses and the harvest time.

Conclusion: Close by sharing Psalm 100, another Psalm of thanksgiving, or a special prayer of thanks.

HANUKKAH   25TH DAY OF KISLEV

This holiday, also called the Feast of Dedication, is the only important Jewish holiday that is not mentioned in the Bible. You can read the story in the first and second books of the Maccabees in the Apocrypha. The Apocrypha, meaning "hidden writings," is a collection of fourteen books not included in the canonization of the Old Testament. It is included in some editions of the Christian Bible and in Roman Catholic Bibles.

Here is a retold version of the story:

The Maccabean revolt took place during the reign of Antiochus IV who succeeded to the throne of Syria in 175 BC. He had a dislike of the Jews in the land of Palestine (a part of the conquered kingdom) because of their distinct way of life and religious practices.

Onias was removed by Antiochus from his role of high priest. A more Greek-minded priest was put in charge and began introducing a radical policy of Hellenization. He had statues introduced to the temple, a gymnasium built, and generally persuaded Jews to adopt Greek ways, including worship of the Greek god Zeus.

The family of Mattathian (nicknamed Maccabees) refused to pay homage to false gods and instead slew the soldier and a Jew who had begun to worship idols. They then fled to the mountains where from hiding places they harried the king's soldiers, eventually defeating them and returning to Jerusalem to cleanse the temple.

It took eight days to remove the hated statues and clean the altars and halls. As the legend goes, the workers could find enough oil to last only one day. Nevertheless, they rekindled the flame above the altar and rededicated the sanctuary. Mysteriously, the temple light (called *Ner Tamid*) continued to burn for a full eight days. Therefore Hanukkah is celebrated for this length of time.

Families today light a *menorah* (a candle holder with eight candles with a ninth in the center which is used as a lighter). On the first night one candle is lit, the second night two, and so on until all are lighted. As part of worship, Psalm 30 is recited and the song, "Rock of Ages," composed originally in the twelfth or thirteenth century, is sung in synagogues.

The *menorah* has an ancient history which predates Hanukkah (see Exodus 25:31-37, 37:17-23). One adorned the temple in Jerusalem and was stolen by Roman soldiers upon its destruction.

During each night of Hanukkah the *menorah* blessing is recited: "Blessed are you, O Lord Our God, ruler of the world who has sanctified us through your *mitzvoth* (commandments) and commanded us to rekindle the Hanukkah lights."

Historically, this was once a minor festival. However, today Hanukah is much beloved, perhaps because of the observance of Christmas and Jewish attempts to counteract all the publicity related to this Christian holiday.

During these eight days children play a DREIDL (drā'dl) game. The *dreidl* is a little top with the letters:

N nothing   G take all   H take half   SH add one (to the pot)

This was originally a gambling game, one of the few times of the year when rabbis of old permitted a game of chance. It serves as a happy game for children.

To play, each player spins the dreidl (dra'dl) in turn. As it stops spinning, the letter which happens to turn up signifies the person's next action: N—do nothing, G—take all goodies in the pot, H—take half the goodies, SH—add one to the pot. (In the "pot" are raisins and nuts.) Play ends when the pot is empty or when a predetermined time is reached. A *dreidl* may be obtained inexpensively at a Jewish synagogue or store.

Dreidl

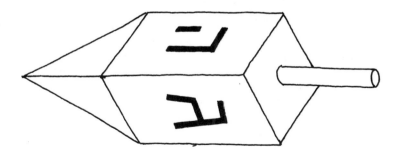

At the family feast, potato pancakes *(latkes)* and dairy foods are eaten. A dubious explanation for latkes suggests that because they are fried in oil one is reminded of the oil lamp. More likely, the custom developed because potatoes are harvested at this time of year.

Latkes (Potato Pancakes)

4	large potatoes (2 cups when grated)	1	tsp. salt
1	carrot	4	tbl. self-rising flour (or 4 tbl. regular flour + 1 tsp. baking powder)
¼	c. grated onion		
2	beaten eggs		

Grate onion, raw potatoes, and carrot and let drain in a sieve for a few minutes. Mix with remaining ingredients. Fry in a heavy frying pan over moderate heat. Serve with honey or applesauce.

GIFTS are exchanged, often one a day, for eight days; and blue is the significant color. Wrapping paper, greeting cards, and frosting on cakes and cookies are all in the symbolic blue.

CELEBRATING HANUKKAH IN SUNDAY SCHOOL SETTINGS

As children arrive, have them either frost homemade or purchased cookies with blue icing or begin to make LATKES. Children can assist by grating potatoes, then measuring and mixing the ingredients. Having an electric hot plate in your room will make it possible to fry them in the classroom.

Children might also draw MENORAHS (a candle holder with nine candles) by using cut-out pieces of construction paper, gold or yellow for holder, white candles, and orange flame. When all have arrived, share the story of Hanukkah. If you have a Bible that contains the Apocrypha, this can also be shown and parts of the story read.

For discussion, ask the class to imagine what would happen if they were suddenly forbidden to attend Sunday school or to worship God and instead were presented with idols or imprisoned as has happened to the Jewish people. How would they react? How easy is it to stand up against oppression? Stress the importance of the religious freedom we so often take for granted.

Play the *dreidl* GAME and serve the refreshment that was planned.

Close by lighting a *menorah*, reciting part of Psalm 30, and saying a prayer of thanks to God for our religious freedom to worship in any way we choose.

The class could also attend a synagogue service and celebration. Many synagogues, when asked, welcome guests. The interaction between Jews and Christians is very meaningful.

JEWISH HOLIDAYS IN FAMILY SETTINGS

As Christians, we should develop an understanding of our Old Testament heritage. This view will help us better understand the New Testament. We also have evidence that Jesus observed many of the Jewish holidays. Indeed, he declared that he came to fulfill the scripture and not to erase it.

Perhaps families might share with children the Jewish holiday traditions and their many connections to Christianity. In many parts of the country, stores sell Jewish holiday items and children become curious about them. Here is an opportunity to share information with them. Family evening Bible readings at each season should include scriptures related to each of these holidays.

Special foods are associated with each one and can be enjoyed by everyone. They may be made at home or purchased in grocery stores and Jewish bakeries.

Purim—*Hamantaschen*   Yom Kippur—*Hallah*
Passover—*Seder* foods, matzos   Succoth—Fresh fruits and
Shavuoth—Cheese blintzes   vegetables
Rosh Hashanah—Honey cake   Hanukkah—*Latkes*

Recipes for each one of these are included in the background pages for the holidays. In addition, it might be enjoyable as well as educational to invite a Jewish friend or neighbor into your home to share one or more of their holidays with your family; attending a synagogue worship service is another idea.

Passover is a good time to participate in a Seder service. Many Christian churches have done this as a part of their congregation's observance of Holy Week. Of course, it might also be an observance of just your family.

JEWISH CALENDAR

The Jewish calendar is made up of 12 lunar months, each of which has 29 or 30 days. To prevent Yom Kippur from falling on the Sabbath (Friday) or Sunday it is possible to alter two of the months, Cheshvan and Kislev. Lunar years have 354 days instead of 365. For this reason it is necessary to have leap years (7 times every 19 years), each of which adds a 13th month.

	1989	1990	1991	1992	1993
Purim	March 21-22	March 11-12	February 28-March 1	March 19-20	March 7-8
Passover	April 20-27	April 10-17	March 30-April 6	April 18-25	April 4-13
Shavuoth	June 9-10	May 30-31	May 19-20	June 7-8	May 26-27
Rosh Hashanah	September 30-Oct 1	September 20-21	September 9-10	September 28-29	September 16-17
Yom Kippur	October 9	September 29	September 18	October 7	September 25
Succoth	October 14-20	October 4-10	September 23-29	October 12-18	September 30
Hanukkah	December 23-30	December 12-19	December 2-9	December 20-27	December 9-16

BIBLIOGRAPHY

The American Book of Days, George William Douglas, revised by Helen Douglas Compton (H.W. Wilson Co., 1948).

The American Book of Days, Jane Hatch (H.W. Wilson Co., revised ed. 1978).

Book of Festival Holidays, Margaret Ickis (Dodd Mead and Co., N.Y., 1964).

Celebrations: The Complete Book of American Holidays, Robert Myers (Doubleday & Co., Garden City, N.J., 1972).

Encyclopedia of Americana (Encyclopedia America Corp., 1957).

Every Day's a Holiday, Ruth Hutchison and Ruth Adams (Harper Bros., N.Y., 1951).

Festivals: Holy Days and Saint Days, Ethel L. Urlin (London, Simpkin, Marshall, Hamilton Kent & Co.; republished by Gale Research Co., Book Tower, Detroit, 1979).

The Jewish Book of Days, Cecil Roth (Herman Press, N.Y., 1966).

Let the Trumpet Sound (M.L. King), Stephen Oates (New American Library, 1982).

The Living Heritage of Passover (Anti-Defamation League of B'nai B'rith, N.Y., undated).

St. Patrick and Irish Christianity, Tom Corfe (Lerner Publications, MN, 1979).